THE ART OF THE MOONSHOT

THE ART OF THE MOONSHOT

THE HIDDEN FACTORS OF EXPONENTIAL SUCCESS

ALYSSA MAVOR

NEW DEGREE PRESS

THE ART OF THE MOONSHOT

THE HIDDEN FACTORS OF EXPONENTIAL SUCCESS

ISBN   978-1-63676-711-6   *Paperback*

          978-1-63730-056-5   *Kindle Ebook*

          978-1-63730-158-6   *Ebook*

CONTENTS

———

INTRODUCTION   1

CHAPTER 1. LEVERS & LEVERAGE   7

CHAPTER 2. UNDERSTANDING THE EXPONENTIAL   17

CHAPTER 3. DIRECTION & MAGNITUDE   31

CHAPTER 4. THE TOOLKIT   47

CHAPTER 5. BIG FISH, SMALL POND   65

CHAPTER 6. THE PARETO PRINCIPLE   79

CHAPTER 7. IN FLOW   91

CHAPTER 8. THE WHISPERS OF CITIES   105

CHAPTER 9. GIVE & TAKE   119

CHAPTER 10. THE BRAIN OUTSIDE YOUR BRAIN   143

CHAPTER 11. MENTAL MODELS   163

CHAPTER 12. THE SECRETS OF SERENDIPITY   179

CHAPTER 13. CHAOS   201

CONCLUSION   217

ACKNOWLEDGMENTS   223

APPENDIX   225

δῶς μοι πᾶ στῶ καὶ τὰν γᾶν κινάσω

*Give me a place to stand and with a
lever I will move the whole world.*

ARCHIMEDES

INTRODUCTION

———

One of the most significant facts about us may finally
be that we all begin with the natural equipment to
live a thousand kinds of life but in the end having
lived only one.

—CLIFFORD GEERTZ

Given just a single shot at existence, we owe it to ourselves to hit the mark.

—JOSHUA ROTHMAN

Once in a while, someone comes along with a particular set
of skills, level of discipline, or amount of luck and changes
the course of history forever. We love to see it. At some level,
humans crave legacy; it's hardwired into our primal drives
to create something that lasts beyond our brief, candlewick
existence before we're snuffed out. Yet, the vast majority of
folks produce their 2.5 offspring and call it a day, leaving the
cycle unchanged. As F. Scott Fitzgerald puts it, "So we beat

on, boats against the current, borne back ceaselessly into the past."[1]

There's something peculiar in how these lives, fully lived, are antithetical to lives imagined. Any four-year-old will gladly articulate how they will be famous or brave or notable in their field, perhaps going to the moon, performing in the New York City Ballet, or saving both the planet and the people as President of the United States. Curious how these fearless dreams are extinguished the closer we get to acquiring the capabilities needed to actually achieve them.

That's not to say we aren't trying. Every day, demand for products and literature on self-improvement and personal achievement increases. The already-mammoth-sized personal development market is expected to surpass $56 billion by 2027.[2] The underlying message, empirically, is—we want to do better. We want to *be* better. Somehow, the disconnect between our current realities and kindergarten ambitions causes a weird kind of mental friction that nags at our attention like a sunburn under denim.

And yet, some of us do thrive. Some thrive so much that they are able to uplift everyone in their vicinity, their nation, or even their species.

The latter is the essence of a moonshot: achieving something so great that it has a resounding impact on the world. It's difficult, sure, but far from impossible. With the right tools, each of us has the capability to achieve success on an exponential scale.

---

1. F. Scott. Fitzgerald, *The Great Gatsby* (New York: Scribner Paperback Fiction, 1995), 138.
2. "Personal Development Market Size Worth $56.66 Billion by 2027," Grand View Research Inc., updated July 27, 2020.

Currently, however, the missing link in the multibillion-dollar self-development industry is the road map. Instead, we're mostly fed platitudes like "make your bed in the morning to feel accomplished." In full transparency, I've read a lion's share of self-help lit and have taken much of it out for a test drive. I've made the green smoothies and eliminated all of the fun foods. I've built a latticework of habit-tracking spreadsheets and regimented my days into neat boxes of time. Digital detoxes—check. Months of low-budget travel—check. Fasting for days—check. I even once took a vow of silence and meditated for a hundred hours in ten days. Though I'm far from the top tail of the bell curve when it comes to courage, stamina, and discipline, I've become somewhat of a dilettante in the self-improvement arts.

The largest lesson that simmered to the top during all of these endeavors was both novel and incredibly obvious: Hard work and self-control do not necessarily equate to exponential success. Standard, linear success is relatively intuitive; we're taught to climb traditional ladders of achievement, trusting that if we just work hard enough, we'll get there. When I first set out to write this book, I believed I could use my learnings and research to help people achieve exponential success. I wanted to give them a ladder. What I eventually realized is that a ladder is a fairly useless tool if you're aiming to achieve a moonshot-level goal. Exponential success requires a vastly different methodology. Even if there was a ladder to the moon, climbing to the top would be so cumbersome and slow that few would likely attempt it.

If we really want to make moonshots, we need a custom rocket, specifically built for our mission. This book is the culmination of everything I've discovered, researched, and learned on the topic. My goal is to provide you with the blueprints and a toolkit to engineer your own rocket—something only you can do. The going might be slow at first, but the ultimate aim is to launch at lightning speed toward the goal you want more than anything else. Certainly, it will be challenging to step back and actually adopt the systems necessary for accelerated success down the line. To do so, we must examine the well-worn pathways of our daily lives and evaluate whether our habits truly align with our end ambitions. It's not easy to release the comfort of our routines. As David Foster Wallace wrote in *Infinite Jest*, "Everything I've ever let go of has claw marks on it."[3]

Releasing these ballasts, however, can be incredibly liberating. In this book, we'll take a look at how we've been setting goals with an ineffective framework for the past forty years, how traditional networking is often backward, and how we're likely spending 80 percent of our time working on the wrong things. We'll take a peek inside Elon Musk's brain, learn how a computer program learns to escape prison, and examine the common habit both John Locke and Kendrick Lamar use to compound their knowledge. If you can muster the will to step off of that linear ladder and use these tools to build a rocket on an exponential trajectory, you're on your way to massive, moonshot-level achievement.

This book is an ode to the possible. It's a deep exploration of science-backed systems and mental models that compound, launching us toward ambitious, exponential success—far and beyond even the kind our four-year-old selves believed in. We'll take a deep dive into practices and tactics that act as force multipliers, empowering us to topple the first

---

3. David Foster Wallace, *Infinite Jest*, (Boston: Little, Brown and Company, 1996), 606.

domino of achievement so that success can begin to cascade and compound on its own. As always, take what resonates with you and scrap the rest. It's your toolkit. Enough with the smoothies and escapism; whatever success looks like to you, you deserve the most of it in the least amount of time.

One thing's for sure. We won't be making beds; we'll be making moonshots.

CHAPTER 1

LEVERS & LEVERAGE

The best way to predict the future is to invent it.

—ALAN KAY

Eureka!

What does it take to change the course of history forever? A naked man, a crown, and some bubbles.

At least, that's what it took for Archimedes to make one of the most profound discoveries in mathematical history. The science behind modern submarines, measurements of bone density, and hot air balloons all came from the ancient Greek polymath's bath-time ruminations.[4] Perhaps bubbles and soap have secret brain-enhancing properties—I won't rule it out—but we wouldn't even have the fabulous exclamation "Eureka!" without these things.

---

4. Rachel Ross, "Eureka! The Archimedes Principle," LiveScience, Future US, updated April 26, 2017.

Archimedes was not a big fan of bathing. In fact, his servants often had to drag the odorous Greek thinker to the bath against his will every month.[5] Still, something in the water seemed to provoke inspiration. Like many of the esteemed geniuses in history, his mind was often in the clouds, making incomprehensible calculations at all hours of the day. According to the philosopher Plutarch, Archimedes would lie in the bath, drawing geometrical figures on his belly. "With his fingers, he drew lines upon his naked body, so far was he taken from himself, and brought into ecstasy or trance, with the delight he had in the study of geometry," Plutarch wrote.[6]

One fateful day, around 267 BCE, Archimedes' amphibious endeavors changed everything. As legend has it, his services were requested by a nearby king to help determine if a goldsmith had cheated him. The king wanted to know if the jeweler had hidden silver inside his supposedly pure-gold crown. Archimedes was assigned to figure out the mystery without damaging the crown; chopping precious jewelry open isn't typically a good policy for preserving value, apparently.[7]

Archimedes stroked his beard and paced about the streets of Syracuse before his trusty servants eventually coerced him into a bath. Perhaps he'd been hitting the olives and cheese a bit hard at the time because in plopping himself into the

5. J. J. O'Connor and E. F. Robertson, "Archimedes—Biography," Maths History, School of Mathematics and Statistics University of St Andrews, updated January 1999.

6. Justin Pollard and Howard Reid, *The Rise and Fall of Alexandria: Birthplace of the Modern Mind*, (Google Books. New York, NY: Viking, 2006), 126.

7. Morris Hickey Morgan, *Vitruvius: The Ten Books on Architecture*, (Harvard University Press, Cambridge, 1914) 253-254, quoted in "The Ten Books On Architecture," The Golden Crown, accessed February 2, 2021.

bath, enough water was displaced to run over the edges and onto the floor.[8]

While most people might sulk or at least "harrumph" about the weight implications, a lightbulb went off inside Archimedes' head. By submerging himself in the water, he saw that the amount of water displaced was equal to the volume of his body. In a moment of triumph, he realized that he could measure the volume of the crown by submerging it in the water and thus determine after weighing the crown if it was lighter than it should be.[9]

Archimedes leapt to his feet, famously bellowing "Eureka!" Ancient Greek for "I found it!"[10] Without bothering to throw on a robe or slip on some sandals, he ran naked through the Syracuse streets, shouting "Eureka!" over and over, bestowing upon the world both a peep show and a mathematical discovery, one of which was enormous enough to make history.

As it turns out, the king had indeed been swindled by the jeweler. Archimedes was celebrated throughout the kingdom. Perhaps he found an even greater fondness for aquatic adventures after that, although no one can be sure.

Archimedes' discovery of how to measure the density of objects with irregular shapes is often paired with a sister discovery he made: the principle of buoyancy. It is speculated that this second principle may have also played a part in the mystery of the crown. In fluid mechanics, the law of buoyancy states that the buoyant force on an object submerged in a fluid is equal to the weight of the fluid that is displaced

---

8.   Mark Salata, "How Taking a Bath Led to Archimedes' Principle," TED, TED-Ed, accessed February 26, 2021.

9.   Ibid.

10. O'Connor and Robertson, "Archimedes—Biography," 1999.

by that object. It is known as Archimedes' principle.[11] Today, both discoveries are used in a wide range of scientific disciplines and help explain everything from why ships float to how to measure the density of teeth.[12]

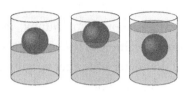

Behind the Curtain

Whether it marks the invention of the lightbulb, the lever, or the Lamborghini, every eureka moment in history has in some way changed the world. Many times, it takes a lifetime's worth of work for an inventor to have their triumphant moment of success.

We'd all love to have a profound revelation like Archimedes and go down in history as one of the great thinkers of our time, but not all of us have fifty years to tinker away and stroke our metaphorical beards in the bath until the epiphany hits. Few of us even have the patience. What, then, does it take to shorten the gap between pursuit and success? How do we expedite the process? These are the questions I've become obsessed with.

I'm not alone in this endeavor. Speedy success is in vogue. These days, startup companies aiming for unicorn status (a

11. "What Is Buoyant Force?" *Khan Academy*, Khan Academy, accessed February 26, 2021.
12. Ross, "Eureka!" 2017.

≥$1 billion valuation) employ buzzword-laden methodologies like "Get Big Fast" and "blitzscaling" to grow as quickly as possible and squash the competition. Likewise, young professionals are joining the Financial Independence Retire Early (FIRE) movement by the thousands in an effort to expedite their plausible retirement age from sixty-five to under forty.[13] While these phenomena have an aura of frenzied excitement, the thought pattern is the same: Scaling success quickly means reaping the benefits for longer.

They may be on to something. Moving with speed allows us to adapt and iterate quickly, filtering out our options to find the best solutions. Considering that 50 percent of people surveyed in an Indeed survey said they'd made at least one dramatic career change in their lives, it makes sense to move fast. If you can switch jobs and quickly rise to the top by taking career leaps instead of running on the same corporate treadmill for forty years, starting over isn't so intimidating.[14] Accelerating success means we can change our circumstances on a dime and succeed in the next venture without skipping a beat.

So, what does it take to accelerate success? Whenever someone achieves exponential success or produces a truly magnificent body of work, I'm always intrigued by the *how*. Perhaps they were endowed with natural talent or brilliance. Maybe they were born with a silver spoon in their mouth and given endless resources and time. Or maybe, just maybe, they achieved the good ol' American Dream by working harder than everyone else.

---

13. Rhiannon Philps, "The Ultimate Guide to the FIRE Movement," *Nerd-Wallet*, NerdWallet Ltd, accessed January 20, 2021.

14. "Career Change Report: An Inside Look at Why Workers Shift Gears," Lead, Indeed, updated October 30, 2019.

What I've come to realize is that these conclusions are unsatisfying. People will always be aided by privilege, exit the womb with prodigious abilities, or simply be handed amazing opportunities in a stroke of luck. Less fortunate folks will work their tail off for their entire creative and professional careers and see very limited success. Knowing this, how do we take agency of our own outcomes? Are we doomed to live a life of mediocrity because we didn't win some genetic lottery?

Not necessarily. Sometimes, someone finds a shortcut. As author Alex Banayan writes, life is really just like a nightclub: There are always three ways in. The first door is the main entrance, where the general public waits in long lines to enter. The second door is the VIP entrance, where billionaires and celebrities stroll through on a red carpet. What no one tells you, though, is that there's always a third option. "It's the entrance where you have to jump out of line, run down the alley, bang on the door a hundred times, crack open the window, and sneak through the kitchen," Banayan writes.[15] According to this theory, people like Bill Gates and Steven Spielberg jump-started their prolific careers early because they found the secret. They took the third door.

Now, while the strategy in Banayan's book, *The Third Door*, largely boils down to brute-force emailing successful people until your keyboard cracks, I've come to believe that there is another way to find these secret passageways. After studying both successful people and companies, a recurring pattern of methodologies for achieving exponential success emerged.

---

15. Alex Banayan, *The Third Door: The Wild Quest to Uncover How the World's Most Successful People Launched Their Careers*, (New York, NY: Currency, 2018) inside cover.

While nothing will guarantee success, it is eminently clear that we can accelerate the possibility of achieving it.

A New Approach

Success means different things to different people. Some folks want to live in the countryside and raise their own chickens. Some aspire to make scientific breakthroughs that change the course of the world. Others want to make funny money and lounge around on yachts in the Maldives for eternity. No matter which flavor of success speaks to you, this book will enumerate practices to achieve a maximum amount of it in a minimal amount of time.

While it may come as a shock to think you could hit your dream goal many times faster than average, it's also unrealistic to think that everyone is moving toward their personal version of success at the same pace. Warren Buffett makes an estimated $1.54 million per hour. At least four people have become Grandmaster chess players before turning thirteen.[16, 17] Ipso facto, third doors exist. Pick the right door, and it will open to an elevator.

Many factors of success are industry-dependent; however, a few common threads exist that successful people employ to tap into exponential growth. This book is not meant to be a prescription but a menu. I won't tell you how to live your life, but I hope to be your moonshot concierge.

---

16. Julia La Roche, "Here's How Much 10 Of The Richest People In The World Made Per Minute In 2013," *Business Insider*, Business Insider, updated December 19, 2013.
17. Isaac Steincamp, "The Youngest Chess Grandmasters In History," Chess. com, updated February 27, 2020.

The Archimedes Lever

Few people in history have achieved exponential success with the same prolificacy as Archimedes. He was a master polymath, making significant contributions as a mathematician, astronomer, engineer, philosopher, physicist, and inventor. He was the first to calculate the number of grains of sand that would fit in the universe. He also infamously designed a war weapon nicknamed *the death ray* that MIT students later proved could burn holes in a ship from one hundred feet away.[18]

Though slightly less sexy than a death ray, one of Archimedes' major accolades was describing the physics of a lever. We've all seen and used levers in daily life, a see-saw being the obvious example. In physics, a lever is categorized as a beam attached to a fixed hinge (fulcrum) that amplifies an input force to produce a greater output force. From bottle openers to tweezers and baseball bats, levers magnify whatever force is put onto them. They're the reason you can jump higher on a diving board than from the pool deck and that it's easier to lift things with a wheelbarrow than with your arms.

Levers are a form of mechanical advantage, or, as we'll call them, force-multipliers.

They concentrate input forces to create greater output forces, which is exactly what this book aims to help you accomplish. We'll investigate the types of force-multipliers that give you the most bang for your buck, effectively launching you toward achieving exponential success. Whether you're a go-getter, a dreamer, a planner, or just plain

---

18. "Archimedes Death Ray," *Ignite*, Massachusetts Institute of Technology, October 2005.

impatient, the end goal is to help you get on the fast track to where you're going.

As Archimedes said, "Give me a place to stand and with a lever I will move the whole world."[19]

These Archimedes levers are all around us, if we know where to look. Let us find our fulcrum and craft our levers. We all deserve a fighting chance at moving the world.

---

19. Chris Rorres, "The Lever Quotations," Archimedes, accessed January 20, 2021.

CHAPTER 2

UNDERSTANDING THE EXPONENTIAL

—

The greatest shortcoming of the human race is our inability to understand the exponential function.

—AL BARTLETT

Nothing in life is to be feared, it is only to be understood. Now is the time to understand more, so that we may fear less.

—MARIE CURIE

Understanding Acceleration

Imagine taking a very thin piece of paper, like the kind they use for Bibles, and folding it in half. It would still be incredibly thin, maybe .002 centimeters. If the paper was somehow resistant to tearing and you had the strength and patience to fold it in half ten times over, it would be about one centimeter thick. Now, bear with me here, how thick do you think the piece of paper would be if you folded it forty-five times? Maybe a few feet? Big enough to sit on like a chair? Long enough to swing around like a Jedi sword?

Actually, it would reach over 230,000 miles, far enough to touch the moon.[20] This is the incredible power of exponential growth. If we hope to harness compounding power to achieve our own moonshot goals, we must understand, to the best of our ability, how exponential functions work. The thing is, humans as a species often severely underestimate their effects. "We have trouble estimating dramatic, exponential change," author Malcolm Gladwell wrote in *The Tipping Point*. "The world—as much as we want it to—does not accord with our intuition."[21]

Certainly, exponential change makes sense on paper. Positive exponential functions on a graph track first to the right before bending sharply upward. When it comes to estimating exponential growth in the real world, though, humans tend to fail miserably. Nature moves slowly, and our glorified monkey minds weren't designed to make sense of the kind of growth that compounds. "Our brains emerged in an era of immediacy, so we're a short-sighted species," Peter H. Diamandis and Steven Kotler write in *The Future Is Faster Than You Think*. "In other words, evolution shaped our time horizons to see about six months into the future."[22]

20. Adrian Paenza, "How Folding Paper Can Get You to the Moon," TED, TED-Ed, accessed February 17, 2021.
21. Malcolm Gladwell, *The Tipping Point: How Little Things Can Make a Big Difference*, (Boston, MA: Little, Brown and Company, 2019), 259.
22. Peter H. Diamandis and Steven Kotler, *The Future Is Faster than You Think: How Converging Technologies Are Transforming Business, Industries, and Our Lives*, (New York, NY: Simon & Schuster, 2020) 231.

Certainly, we can plan more than six months in advance for one-time events, like going on vacation. We can even predict growth with some relative success—when it's linear. If you are painting a mural at a steady pace, you can loosely predict when you will be done. When it comes to exponential growth, however, we often fail spectacularly. Ever notice how home building projects and real estate developments run way over schedule and over budget? This is because many of the individual tasks within the larger project compound on one another. Humans have a hilariously difficult time estimating compounding effects. We tie our brains into knots attempting to predict the outcome of a paper-folding exercise, let alone picturing something like the size of our ever-expanding universe.

Still, examples of exponential growth are all around us. The most notable one in the past century is the acceleration of technology.

Moore's Law

For the past fifty years, computers have become twice as fast and twice as cheap about every 18-24 months, corresponding directly to the size and speed of microchips.[23] Very fast computer processors can now fit inside small cell phones, and they are incredibly affordable compared to models made just a few decades before. If you don't want to pay half a million dollars to own a computer the size of your garage that can only accomplish basic tasks, like the ones in the early seventies, you're benefiting from a concept called Moore's Law.

---

23. *Encyclopedia Britannica*, s.v. "Moore's Law," accessed February 16, 2021.

Moore's Law, the eponymous principle observed by Intel cofounder Gordon E. Moore, refers specifically to the trend that microchips gain twice as many transistors each year or two while the price of computers as a whole decreases by half.[24] For the most part, this concept has held true in much of technology: It gets faster, cheaper, and smaller over time, and the rate of change is exponential.

Remember, exponential growth means the *growth* is *growing*. Each year, the rate of change gets *faster*.

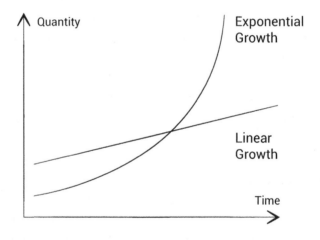

Thanks to this acceleration, anyone can write a blog post that reaches a hundred thousand people, communicate instantly with someone across the globe, or secure a remote job in the next twenty-four hours, none of which would be possible even three decades ago.

---

24. Carla Tardi, "Moore's Law Explained," *Investopedia*, Investopedia, September 16, 2020.

Comprehending this change is also where it gets tricky. Ray Kurzweil, futurist and author of *The Singularity Is Near,* summed up the acceleration phenomena:

> When people think of a future period, they intuitively assume that the current rate of progress will continue for future periods. However, careful consideration of the pace of technology shows that the rate of progress is not constant... Our memories are nonetheless dominated by our very recent experience.[25]

Try as we might, we mostly look at the world with a linear lens, because up until the past fifty-something years, that's how everything progressed. Diamandis and Kotler write,

> Your great-great-great-grandfather's life was roughly the same as his great-great-grandson's life. But now we live in a world that is global and exponential... Forget about the difference between generations; currently mere months can bring a revolution. Your brain— which hasn't really had a hardware update in two hundred thousand years—wasn't designed for this scale or speed.[26]

We are just now reaching the inflection point in history when the graph starts to curve up and to the right. It's tough to see what's next. "Exponential models are not straight. They are like a bend in the road that prevents you from seeing around the corner," Shift Thinking CEO Mark Bonchek wrote in

25. Ray Kurzweil, "The Law of Accelerating Returns," *Kurzweil Accelerating Intelligence,* Kurzweil Network, March 7, 2001.
26. Diamandis and Kotler, *The Future Is Faster than You Think,* 12.

Harvard Business Review.[27] Though we don't typically recommend for drivers to go full-speed around blind curves, it's exactly what we're doing every day.

People who learn to identify compounding effects can begin to harness them and shape them, intentionally crafting their futures rather than allowing life to happen to them. The key understanding is that compounding effects don't just happen sometimes; they're happening all around us, all the time. When we choose to cook at home and forego that $60 restaurant meal, we may forget that the $60 invested at a 6 percent return rate could bloom into $600 in forty years. If you've met your caloric limit for the day, one extra cup of ice cream every night for a year has the potential to bestow on your waistline an extra twenty-eight pounds, about the same weight as fifteen boxes of spaghetti or one Icelandic sheepdog.[28, 29] Compounding doesn't discriminate. It happens positively or negatively with any choice we make repeatedly.

A classic example of the mind-boggling power of exponential growth is the wheat and chessboard problem. Legend has it that a mythical figure called Sissa ibn Dahir approached King Shirham of India around 500 CE and presented him with the first game of chess. The king, so delighted at the new invention, ordered chess boards to be placed in temples around the kingdom.[30]

---

27. Mark Bonchek, "How to Create an Exponential Mindset," *Harvard Business Review*, Harvard Business Review, October 4, 2017.

28. "Calories in 1 Cup of Ice Cream and Nutrition Facts," *FatSecret*, FatSecret, accessed March 5, 2021.

29. "13 Common Items That Weigh About 30 Pounds," *Weight of Stuff*, Weight of Stuff, August 23, 2020.

30. Ibn Khallikan, *Ibn Khallikan's Biographical Dictionary*, translated by William MacGuckin de Slane, *Google Books* 3. Vol. 3, 1970.

The king wanted to repay Sissa for his fantastic invention. "Ask me for whatever you desire," he said to Sissa, clearly miscalculating the brahmin.[31] Sissa humbly requested to be repaid in grains of wheat. He asked that a single grain of wheat be placed in the first square of his chessboard, two grains in the second, four grains in the third, and so forth, doubling each time until the board was filled. After laughing off the suggestion as too little repayment, the king was soon informed by his accountants that not enough wheat existed in the whole kingdom so as to fill the board.[32]

In fact, the total amount Sissa requested was over 18 quintillion wheat grains, several times the amount of wheat harvested in the world over several decades. Yikes.

I'd like to think that I am immune to such ill forethought; however, I too was duped like King Shirham at one point. As a child, I owned a book of fun facts and science experiment ideas. One of my favorite sections of the book was a page called "Want to Win a Million Dollars?" The cardboard page had about fifty circular indents in it the size of pennies, and, just like Sissa, the instructions directed me to put one penny in the first indent, two in the second, four in the next, then eight, doubling the amount each time.

---

31. Ibid.
32. Ibid.

The authors promised to write a check for a million dollars to anyone who could fill the whole board with pennies. Scrutinizing my piggy bank, it took me a long time to realize I'd never make it past the first row of indents on the page. Only years later did I realize that anyone who did fill it out would be sending more than $1 million to the authors in the first place. The final amount to fill the board would actually have been worth about $11,258,999,068,426. Something tells me my piggy bank wasn't equipped to handle that kind of capital.

Why We Fail

The paradox of comprehending exponential growth is coming to terms with the fact that even if we think we understand it, we don't typically estimate its effects with any accuracy. A study in the Journal of Exponential Psychology demonstrated that people are overconfident about their ability to understand and calculate exponential growth.[33] Participants in the study were wrong in their exponential estimates far more frequently than they believed, even when they used spreadsheets to help them with estimations.

The logical solution to this issue is to give people better tools to help them understand the magnitude of this kind of growth, which can be helpful for tasks like managing money. Frustratingly, however, the scientists noted that "individuals have suboptimally low demand for tools and services that could improve their financial decisions."[34] Like unruly tod-

---

33. Matthew R. Levy and Joshua Tasoff, "Exponential-Growth Bias and Overconfidence," *Journal of Economic Psychology* 58 (February 2017): 1-14.
34. Ibid.

dlers, we insist we understand something clearly beyond our means and refuse assistance when it is available.

This variety of personal oversight isn't limited to non-scientists. Even experts vastly underestimate the power of accelerating progress. Kurzweil, an expert in the acceleration of tech space and owner of a modest twenty-one honorary doctorates, once rebuked a Nobel Prize-winning panelist for supposing we won't see self-replicating artificial intelligence entities (think: technology that is smarter than us) in the next century.[35]

"I pointed out that one hundred years was indeed a reasonable estimate of the amount of technical progress required to achieve this particular milestone at today's rate of progress," Kurzweil said, "But because we're doubling the rate of progress every decade, we'll see a century of progress—at today's rate—in only twenty-five calendar years."[36] By Kurzweil's estimate, the panelist had miscalculated by about seven decades. Oof.

The implications of this variety of acceleration are incredible. Think about your ten-year plan. What if, with the proper systems and principles, you could reduce the time gap to your goals by 75 percent? You'd reach your decade-long goals in two and a half years and have another seven and a half years of accelerated-progress time to surpass them further than you ever believed.

In order to reach this level of success, we must recognize that the three-odd pounds of gray tissue inside our skulls won't be able to anticipate the end result. That's not exactly the important part. Like launching a rocket, our responsibility is to simply get it into the air and let its own systems

---

35. Kurzweil, "The Law," 2001.
36. Ibid.

take over. Knowing this, we can still build the launchpad and aim for the stars.

Eroom's Law

Now, we know that technology and progress are accelerating faster than ever. Human achievement is moving at warp speed compared to just a few hundred years ago, and more people on planet Earth are living healthy, happy lives than ever before in history. So what's the hang-up? Why worry about exponential personal growth instead of kicking back with martinis and watching the world speed toward the pinnacle of human success?

Well, for starters, we're creating problems at the same pace as we're fixing them. For each advancement we make, we tend to create equal-and-opposite negative externalities.

Solar panels are one example of a bright invention with a potentially dark footprint. According to the US Energy Information Administration, toxic materials are used to create the photovoltaic cells in panels. Some solar thermal systems use potentially hazardous fluids that can significantly damage the surrounding environment if they leak. Clearing land to construct a solar panel system on the ground also damages ecosystems. Even when panels last for a few decades, they can be extremely difficult to recycle at the end of their working lifespan. Much of the time, they go to waste, potentially releasing toxins like lead and cadmium into the surrounding environment.[37] It's estimated that solar panel waste could

---

37. "Solar Explained," Solar Energy and the Environment, U.S. Energy Information Administration, updated September 23, 2020.

reach 78 million metric tons by 2050, about one and a half times the weight of the Great Wall of China, the heaviest thing ever built by humans.[38, 39]

Cell phones are another Jekyll and Hyde example of human advancement. The mineral components in cell phones and computer technology have been dubbed *blood minerals* due to the human rights violations often committed during the mining process.[40] Cell phone use has also been correlated with worsening anxiety, depression, and insomnia in adolescents.[41] From distracted driving to social isolation, we cannot assuredly say that the introduction of pocket-sized smart technology has been a net-positive.

Don't get me wrong, I benefit from both solar energy and cell phone use. But we need to recognize the pace of negative acceleration as we crystallize our conviction to pursue positive acceleration. From cars and fossil fuels to social media and cyberbullying, most every technological advancement in history has come with its own set of issues. This is an example of Eroom's law, Moore's law in reverse. Moore's law states that technology is getting faster and cheaper, exponentially. Eroom's law suggests that progress is actually slowing down, each new system exhibiting more bugs than features.

Researchers studying Eroom's law found that the research and development of new pharmaceuticals has doubled in cost about every decade since 1950. For every billion dollars

38. Michael Shellenberger, "If Solar Panels Are So Clean, Why Do They Produce So Much Toxic Waste?" *Forbes*, Forbes, updated May 28, 2019.
39. Thomas C. Frohlich and John Harrington, "The Heaviest Objects in the World," *MSN News*, Microsoft News, updated May 11, 2018.
40. David Zax, "Is Your Cell Phone Helping to Fund a Civil War?" Smithsonian.com, Smithsonian Institution, updated October 1, 2013.
41. Sehar Shoukat, "Cell Phone Addiction and Psychological and Physiological Health in Adolescents," *EXCLI Journal* 18 (February 4, 2019): 47-50.

spent, the number of new drugs approved has been cut in half.[42] Many theories attempt to explain this, from the lowered risk tolerance of regulating agencies today to the low-hanging-fruit problem of all the easy options already having been found.

Many of the low-hanging fruits of innovation indeed have been discovered, patented, and marketed already. It's unfortunately too late for any of us to make $500 million from a blanket-sweatshirt combo, like the Snuggie, or create a fortune from selling pet rocks.[43]

To stay ahead of the curve of new world issues created by human advancement and ensure continual innovation toward a better world, society has more of a need than ever for exponentially successful individuals. We need the big thinkers, the bold doers, and the intrepid creators to carry us forward.

Whether the negative aspects of success are accelerating exponentially, as in pharmaceuticals, or in more of a linear fashion, it stands to reason that we should aim to create solutions and positive inventions on an exponential timeline. Either we'll end up exactly matching pace in a 1-for-1 race with the world's problems, or we'll far surpass them, creating a healthier and more equitable world.

One thing's for certain: It's pretty hard to reach a world-changing level of success without having a lever of some kind to lift you up. "Making small changes to things that already exist might lead you to a local maximum, but it won't help you find the global maximum," Peter Thiel said

---

42. Kaigham J. Gabriel, "How to Fight 'Eroom's Law,'" *Scientific American Blog Network, Scientific American*, updated July 9, 2019.

43. Annie Nova, "10 Unlikely Products That Made Millions of Dollars," *CNBC*, CNBC, updated December 11, 2017.

in *Zero to One*.[44] We must pursue the massive changes, using exponential growth, to help us reach our moonshot goals. In the next chapter, we'll discuss Sam Altman's deceptively simple formula for impact, take a peek behind the curtain at Google's moonshot factory, and explore the importance of both passion and failure when it comes to exponential success.

44. Peter Thiel, *Zero to One: Notes on Startups, or How to Build the Future*, (London: Virgin Books, 2014) 78.

CHAPTER 3

DIRECTION & MAGNITUDE

The gods of the Greeks were like helpless children compared to humankind today and the powers we now wield.

— MIHALY CSIKSZENTMIHALYI

The Art of the Moonshot

Chasing exponential growth involves a paradox. You must be systematic and disciplined enough to invest your time in long-term change but open-minded enough to believe in the impossible.

Giant *shoot-for-the-moon* goals are a perfect target to aim for if you're hoping to achieve exponential success. We'll call them personal moonshots, borrowing from Google's "moonshot factory," the arm that creates products to solve possibly impossible problems. This kind of goal is a unique blend of optimism and logic that bridges the gap between possible and probable.

Choosing a focal point, a personal moonshot, provides clarity so you aren't blindly stumbling toward an unknown goal.

The inherent challenge with moonshots is that they can seem almost absurdly out of reach. These goals are the opposite of low-hanging fruits. If they were easy, they would have been done before. Still, those seeking exponential success must often chart unexplored territory to experience enormous rewards. Elon Musk is considered an oddity for wanting to colonize Mars, eliminate our reliance on fossil fuels, and implant medical microchips into our brains. And yet, he has come closer than anyone else in the history of the world to doing all three of those things.

Still, if you're anything like me, logical goals are the easiest to digest. It's terrifying to proclaim that you're aiming to do something grandiose. The only results of that kind of statement seem to be looking like a fool or humiliating failure. No, thanks. I'll sit at home with my book and my coffee and adopt stray cats for the next forty years.

But, at the risk of sounding cliché, where would we be without the dreamers? We certainly wouldn't have computers, cars, electric light bulbs, and space travel. We wouldn't have access to avocados and pineapples year-round in Montana if someone hadn't figured out the complex supply chain. We wouldn't even have the Snuggie. Each one of those things required someone to take a leap of faith, risk looking like an idiot, and keep after their mission with dogged perseverance until their idea gained traction.

We must metabolize that chasing an enormous goal is going to feel unnatural at first, particularly to logic-lovers like me, who tend to plan their lives on a linear timeline. "Linear thinking is organized, rule-based, logical, and easy to replicate," writes Amy Blacklock of *Women Who Money*. "It draws a straight line from here to there. Society teaches us to think linearly. But when you think linearly, you underestimate what's actually possible with time."[45]

Exponential success requires breaking free of the linear mindset. Jim Collins, business researcher and author of *Good to Great* and *Built to Last*, encourages entrepreneurs to set their ambitions terrifyingly high. He coined the term BHAGs (*bee-hags*), meaning Big Hairy Audacious Goals, to describe these moonshot dreams.[46] Collins and his research team studied the secret sauce behind successful, visionary companies. Their research found that visionary companies chase BHAGs more often than comparison companies. The most successful and impactful companies weren't afraid to look stupid by chasing something hairy and audacious.[47]

BHAGs don't need to be explained, Collins writes. They produce a gut feeling in anyone who hears about them. This kind of feeling can unite a startup company's team, or even a whole nation. President Kennedy's 1961 proclamation that he would help land a man on the moon was a BHAG. Assertive and poignant, the literal moonshot goal was clear as day and helped propel the American people toward achieving the formerly impossible mission. It resonated instantly with anyone who heard it.

The more we see others chase their moonshots, the less daunting it seems to set a BHAG. Mo Gawdat, former chief business officer at Google's "moonshot factory," Google

---

45. Amy Blacklock, "How to Achieve an Exponential Mindset," *Wealthfit*, accessed January 7, 2021.

46. Jim Collins and Jerry I Porras, "BHAG—Big Hairy Audacious Goal," *Jim Collins*, Jim Collins, accessed January 13, 2021.

47. Ibid.

X, is used to chasing after audacious goals. According to Gawdat, employees were encouraged to think on massive, earth-shattering scales. "I think Google X became what it is because we wouldn't settle for a 10 percent, 20 percent, 100 percent improvement on something, but we would shoot for a 10x improvement," he said.[48] Google X's current endeavors include using computer vision to map marine wildlife in the ocean, giving four billion people access to the internet with beams of light, and creating sundry classically futuristic inventions like self-driving cars and smart contact lenses.[49]

Gawdat spent years working on world-changing moonshots within the company, but it wasn't until tragedy struck that he discovered his own personal BHAG.

In 2014, Gawdat's son Ali went in for a routine operation and tragically passed away.[50] Seventeen days after the heart-breaking event, Gawdat sat down to write about happiness. Solving the formula for happiness was an endeavor they had worked on together. Shortly after the tragedy, Gawdat decided to dedicate his life to a moonshot in honor of Ali: making a billion people happy.[51]

Gawdat has since left Google to spend his time researching and writing about happiness. He wrote a bestselling book on the topic, *Solve for Happy,* and now runs workshops

---

48. Mo Gawdat, "How One Google Engineer Turned Tragedy into a Moonshot," HBR IdeaCast, *Harvard Business Review,* updated January 2, 2019.
49. "Projects," X, the Moonshot Factory, X Development LLC, accessed March 5, 2021.
50. Ian Tucker, "Google's Mo Gawdat: 'Happiness Is like Keeping Fit. You Have to Work out'," *The Guardian,* Guardian News and Media, updated April 30, 2017.
51. Mo Gawdat, "The Mission," A Billion People Happy. Onebillionhappy, updated June 18, 2019.

through his organization, One Billion Happy. As an engineer, pivoting toward such a different goal was unprecedented. But since when was there a precedent for changing the world?

How to Choose a Moonshot

When selecting your moonshot, it's important to consider the impact you wish to have. We all have the ability to shift the course of history with our Archimedes levers, making positive change useful at any size. But different people will prefer to work on projects of varying scales. In the true spirit of moonshots, we'll explore impact on a large scale.

Sam Altman knows a thing or two about impact. As former president of Silicon Valley's darling, the startup incubator Y Combinator, and current CEO of OpenAI, the company he co-founded with Elon Musk, Altman has had the kind of impact on business and tech in ways most people can only dream of. Directly and indirectly, Altman and his peers have shaped many of the most important technological innovations that have emerged in the last two decades. How does one create this kind of impact? Altman believes it can be distilled into a simple calculation. "The expected value of your impact on the world is like a vector," he said. "It is defined by two things: direction and magnitude. That's it."[52]

---

52. Sam Altman (@sama), "The expected value of your impact on the world is like a vector," Twitter, August 24, 2020, 9:04 p.m.

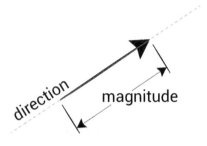

Direction must come first. Moonshots necessitate singular attention toward one goal, endeavor, or final product. So picking a lane, at least for a period of time, is a crucial piece to the puzzle. In later chapters, we'll explore why rules like the Pareto Principle and conditions like flow state rely on singular focus. For now, consider that one mental target is generally just easier.

That said, choosing just one thing to focus your time and energy on is a daunting prospect for many people, this author included. I've made a habit of putting an egg in every possible basket rather than risk hoarding them all in one place. With so many opportunities, career paths, hobbies, and options, choosing one direction can be challenging. This may explain why, in my adolescence, I fled from greatness like it would scald me if I touched it. In lieu of sticking with one hobby or sport and gaining proficiency, I dabbled in swimming, pottery, horseback riding, playing the trumpet, hip hop dance, speech and debate, student council, yoga, snowboarding, and more. When I made it to the varsity teams in soccer, tennis, and rock climbing, respectively, I quit all of them at the peak of my ability. Too afraid to actually dedicate myself to one thing, I evaded any possible greatness being thrust upon me like Neo dodged bullets in *The Matrix*.

The psychological trap I fell into is known as maximizing. In my search to find something I was best at, I didn't stay for long in any one endeavor. In a world where the theoretical perfect job is five hundred LinkedIn posts away or the perfect partner is two thousand Tinder swipes away, young people, in particular, have been conditioned to search for perfect instead of good enough. With such immense optionality, settling for something less than perfect is so counterintuitive it's almost painful. Of course, truly perfect options are largely fictional, leading many maximizers to find themselves on a hamster wheel of analysis paralysis.

Choosing a direction requires finding the *good enough* option, lest we dally long enough that the train leaves without us. Finding the satisfactory and sufficient, but not perfect, option is known as "satisficing," a portmanteau developed by US Nobel Prize-winning economist Herbert A. Simon.[53] According to Simon, evolution designed animals to be satisficers in order to survive. "Evidently, organisms adapt well enough to 'satisfice'; they do not, in general, 'optimize,'" he wrote in his 1956 paper, "Rational Choice and the Structure of the Environment."[54] In nature, organisms seek to balance effort with reward. As it turns out, the lioness who maximized her hunt for the best gazelle, rather than killing the available one, didn't sufficiently succeed in feeding her cubs.

Indeed, the current generation of maximizers is facing hefty consequences. In one study of adolescents, researchers discovered a more-means-worse phenomenon in young people searching for love using online dating platforms.

53. Adam Waude, "Maximizers vs. Satisficers: Who Makes Better Decisions?" *Psychologist World*, Psychologist World, December 14, 2016.
54. Herbert A. Simon, "Rational Choice and the Structure of the Environment." *Psychological Review* 2 (1956): 129-38.

The maximizers of the group, who insisted on finding their Prince/Princess Charming, spent excessive time looking for partners, at their own peril. According to the study, this flavor of maximizing behavior "leads to worse choices by reducing users' cognitive resources, distracting them with irrelevant information, and reducing their ability to screen out inferior options." Maximizing adolescents had worse luck than the satisficers, who were happy to accept matches that were *good enough* and met a basic standard of their criteria. Counterintuitively, the participants who tried hardest had the least success.[55]

Instead of ending up in the vortex of indecision when choosing your moonshot goal, it makes sense to satisfice and choose a goal that fulfills the basic principles that are important to you, like purpose, feasibility, and interest. Keep in mind that your moonshot doesn't have to be the only thing you do in life. Altman recommends picking a goal with a "long-but-not-too-long timescale," about 10-20 years.[56] Certainly, incredible and lasting success can happen faster than this, but deeply committed people are willing to sink their teeth in and fight if it takes longer.

If you're still averse to this kind of commitment, you may be barking up the wrong tree. As writer Nat Eliason put it, "Commitment is a bad word. It suggests fighting yourself to act against your impulses. It suggests doing something 'because you should.' That's not motivating, though, and focusing on commitment runs up against the maximization impulses we know we have. Instead, forget commitment.

---

55. Mu-Li Yang and Wen-Bin Chiou, "Looking Online for the Best Romantic Partner Reduces Decision Quality: The Moderating Role of Choice-Making Strategies," *CyberPsychology & Behavior* 13 (April 2009).

56. Altman, Twitter Post, August 24.

Think about what you want to invest in."[57] Don't be committed. Be dedicated. Be invested. Be passionate.

What about Passion?

There's much ado about loving your work, and different philosophies abound. Half of the traditional career literature urges people to follow their hearts, promising that the money will follow. The other half encourages people to follow the money and pursue passion projects in their free time.

With so many factors at play—money, location, prestige, training, pride, accessibility—job priorities will be different for everyone.

It remains, however, that an average American will spend roughly ninety thousand hours, or one-third of their life, at work.[58] Finding something you're passionate about will make these hours immensely more productive and enjoyable than spending them doing something you hate. There's nobility in doing necessary work. There's privilege in choosing to follow your heart. Acknowledging this, those who are afforded the ability to do what they love have an advantage. No one will fight harder for something than what is meaningful to them. Very few people who have changed the world for the better have done it accidentally.

Now, following your passion takes on different forms.

There is a term in Japanese for something that keeps a person going: *ikigai*. Though there's no direct English translation,

57. Nat Eliason, "Forget Commitment: Invest in Something," Nat Eliason, updated December 1, 2020.
58. "One Third of Your Life Is Spent at Work," News, Gettysburg College, accessed January 11, 2021.

it essentially means, "the reason you get up in the morning," or raison d'être. Ikigai is often portrayed in a Venn diagram with four overlapping circles: what you love, what you are good at, what the world needs, and what you can be paid for.[59] The intersection of all four bubbles, they say, is your purpose in life.

Places in the world with an emphasis on purpose, well-being, and ikigai correspond with blue zones, or longevity hotspots. Scientists are now discovering that psychological factors like meaning and ikigai have a strong correlation with expected

59. Yukari Mitsuhashi, "Ikigai: A Japanese Concept to Improve Work and Life," *BBC Worklife*, BBC, updated August 7, 2017.

lifespan.[60] Finding a deeper meaning in your work can be good for your body as well as your soul and is a good thing to keep in mind when selecting your moonshot. Due to the length of time it often takes for these goals to come to fruition, anything that increases your endurance and willingness to persevere is an advantage.

Magnitude

The second half of Altman's equation for impact, after direction, is magnitude. Nature might have us think that tackling something bigger is proportionally more difficult. Indeed, scaling Mount Everest is much harder than summiting Pikes Peak. Certainly, I'd rather get in a fight with a squirrel instead of a grizzly bear. But outside of the physical world, larger doesn't necessarily mean more difficult.

Entrepreneur Naveen Jain believes more people should tackle moonshots, and that they might actually be deceivingly less hard than we think. Bigger goals may not be largely more challenging than smaller goals. Jain writes:

> Because the goal is to achieve something that is an order of magnitude greater than what exists today, it doesn't necessarily follow that it will be an order of magnitude more difficult than, say, aiming for something that is just 10 percent better. That's not a moonshot. If the limits of your vision constrain you to creating something that's merely 10 percent better, 10

60. Michaéla C. Schippers and Niklas Ziegler, "Life Crafting as a Way to Find Purpose and Meaning in Life," *Frontiers in Psychology* 10, no. 2778, accessed January 12, 2021.

percent faster, or 10 percent cheaper, then you're operating in the biggest possible sphere of competition.[61]

High-magnitude dreams automatically place you outside the main battleground of competition. Aiming to create something that is 10 percent better than what currently exists, as an end goal, is not ideal (and probably not a moonshot), but creating a company that grows its revenue at 10 percent per week can have astonishing results over time. A company that makes just $100 a week growing 10 percent weekly would generate a whopping $15 billion in annual revenue after just three years. That's the power of compounding growth. This kind of growth isn't necessarily hyperbolic; Y Combinator companies are expected to grow at 5 to 7 percent weekly, with 10 percent being the goal.[62]

Reaching these milestones of exponential success doesn't have to be excruciatingly difficult from day one. Compounding growth is slow, then sudden. Before the dramatic explosion, growth happens on a very gradual basis, and until momentum picks up, it's important to just focus on laying the groundwork.

Altman, who has now funded or mentored many of the major new companies in the tech world, actually believes that the harder a startup company idea is, the greater its chance of succeeding. While it's easy to gain momentum with a basic-idea startup, it's much harder to gain the support of people who will believe in and support your mission over the long run. "An easy startup is a headwind; a hard startup

---

61. Naveen Jain and John Schroeter, *Moonshots: Creating a World of Abundance* (New York: Moonshots Press, 2018), 16.
62. "How Fast Should You Be Growing?" *TechCrunch*, TechCrunch, updated August 24, 2013.

is a tailwind," he said.[63] In other words, the moonshots tend to win while the basic small-dream startups often fail.

Business-related or not, choosing the moonshot project over the easy endeavor can be beneficial. Moonshots are most often driven by a larger mission, and people congregate over purpose and the promise of something great. Even if your moonshot rocket crashes and burns, you'll have a cohort of people who believe in you and who will support you in the next endeavor.

Failure

Of course, there will likely be hundreds of little failures on the path to achieving your moonshot goal, and perhaps a few enormous ones as well. I'll do us all a favor here and not quote Thomas Edison, but you can expect to hit some serious obstacles on your way to success.

Jim Collins calls moonshot goals "Big Hairy Audacious Goals," precisely because they are so terrifying to undertake. One of the biggest psychological obstacles to overcome in chasing a personal moonshot is the fear of failure, a fear directly tied to the ego and its resistance to looking bad in the eyes of others.

Mo Gawdat, the Googler-turned-happiness-entrepreneur, believes ego is one of the main impediments to people chasing their moonshot. Pride either prevents people from trying new and innovative things or makes them resistant to admitting failure.

---

63. Sam Altman, "The Strength of Being Misunderstood," *Sam Altman* (blog), updated February 26, 2020.

At Google X, people were praised for closing down projects that weren't viable instead of shamed for failing. "It was deemed to be the brave thing to do to admit that something didn't work," Gawdat said. The CEO, Astro Teller, would sometimes pop champagne and give bonuses to teams who had decided to close the door on failed projects.[64]

As a result, the fear of failure didn't stop people from pursuing wildly ambitious, even ludicrous, projects, many of which the company keeps confidential.

Gawdat, now on his personal moonshot mission to help a billion people find happiness, is simultaneously working on an inner goal: letting go of his ego. "If you drop your ego and focus on who you really are and what you can do with that person that you are, there's going to be something that is amazing that you can uniquely achieve that no one else can achieve," he said.[65]

The best way to mitigate a fear of failure is to go into the goal knowing and accepting that a series of mini-failures will happen. You'll reach a lot of dead ends before you find the path. You'll likely make some big, public, embarrassing mistakes. You'll lose money. You'll disappoint people.

Surrounding yourself with people who understand these facts is paramount. Joining forces with people who have failed in the past means they will be more empathetic to your journey. This is one of the reasons "So, how many failed companies have you started?" is such a common opener at cocktail parties and in Tinder messages in the Bay Area. Venture capitalists even sometimes prefer to invest in founders who have failed at previous startups because they know they

---

64. Gawdat, "How One Google Engineer," 2019.
65. Ibid.

have learned from their mistakes. When failure becomes a badge of honor, the associated fear starts to dissipate. In the next chapter, we'll look at additional tools to mitigate fear. But knowing that you will absolutely fail in some capacity is a good mindset to cultivate.

The Bottom Line

So, why do it? Why choose a personal moonshot? A better question might be why not? Everyone wants to make their mark on the world in some capacity. Arguably, everyone who can, should. The final words of Steve Jobs' 2005 Stanford commencement address were, "Stay hungry. Stay foolish."[66] If you're reading this, you intend to do just that.

---

66. "Text of Steve Jobs' Commencement Address (2005)," *Stanford News,* Stanford University, updated June 12, 2017.

CHAPTER 4

THE TOOLKIT

Nothing in this world can take the place of persistence. Talent will not: Nothing is more common than unsuccessful men with talent. Genius will not: Unrewarded genius is almost a proverb. Education will not: The world is full of educated derelicts. Persistence and determination alone are omnipotent.

—CALVIN COOLIDGE

Let's be honest. Chasing after a really big dream can suck.

Just ask someone who perhaps knows more about sucking than anyone on the planet: Sir James Dyson, inventor of vortex suction technology and the Dyson vacuum. Before his invention took off, Dyson created 5,127 vacuum prototypes. It took him fifteen years.[67]

The whole family made sacrifices for him. "By the time I made my fifteenth prototype, my third child was born. By

---

67. James Dyson, "No Innovator's Dilemma Here: In Praise of Failure," *Wired*, Conde Nast, September 11, 2018.

2,627, my wife and I were really counting our pennies. By 3,727, my wife was giving art lessons for some extra cash," Dyson says. "These were tough times, but each failure brought me closer to solving the problem. It wasn't the final prototype that made the struggle worth it. The process bore the fruit. I just kept at it."[68]

Dyson Ltd. is now a billion-dollar company that sells all kinds of electronics. James Dyson also runs a foundation to help other inventors, young and old, achieve their dreams.[69]

So, how did Dyson achieve such enormous success? He had a specific goal in mind and was positively unrelenting on his quest to achieve it.

Not So SMART Goals

Now, several different methods exist for setting goals, and the technique can make a huge difference in your ability to stick with and accomplish them. The most common goal-setting framework is SMART, which stands for specific, measurable, achievable, relevant, and timely.[70] Many people have seen this acronym scattered around the web, read it in self-help books, and even learned it at their jobs. It was part of the lesson plan several times during my high school career and several times again in college.

This framework has withstood the test of time and to its credit, it seems logical and intuitive. But how come so many

---

68. Ibid.
69. "Engineering The Future," The James Dyson Foundation, The James Dyson Foundation North America, accessed March 6, 2021.
70. "Goal Setting," MIT Human Resources, Massachusetts Institute of Technology, accessed February 3, 2021.

people who follow these steps to create their goals still don't succeed? Are moonshot goals necessarily specific, measurable, achievable, relevant, and timely? If we take a closer look, it becomes apparent that perhaps SMART isn't so smart at all.

Upon closer inspection, the SMART framework may actually be an Achilles' heel to your personal moonshot project. Let's talk about the third word: achievable. The risky but inherent quality about moonshots is that they are *shoot for the moon* goals. Nine out of ten times, they haven't been done before, so there's no track record to follow. If you, like Mo Gawdat, want to make a billion people in the world happy, how do you necessarily know if it is *achievable*? If you'd like to break a Guinness World Record, write the next *Harry Potter* series, or solve world hunger, you have no way of knowing exactly if it's possible to accomplish. Yet, anyone who has attempted these goals has made progress simply in the act of trying. Of course, you believe in your goal; you wouldn't pursue it otherwise. But using *achievable* as a metric disqualifies the *possibly possible* goals that can ultimately turn into successful moonshots.

Another issue with the SMART framework is the word *timely*, sometimes written as time-constricted. Keeping a goal timely means setting a deadline, like, "I want to run ten miles by April 1st," or "I'm going to practice coding for forty-five minutes a day for thirty days." While having a clear window for completion works well with short-term goals, it tends to fall flat with big, earth-shattering goals. The longer the timeframe for a goal, the harder it is to estimate. People with true moonshot ambitions tend to fill in the gap with vague phrases like "before I die" or "in my lifetime," rendering the *timely* characteristic rather useless. The most profound achievements may even involve laying the framework for the next generation to build upon and can't be limited to a certain time period at all. Timely isn't a great metric for setting enormous goals, but it can be used as a tactic to complete smaller steps on the way to get there.

Relevant is not necessarily a helpful guideline for setting goals, either, writes Anne-Laure Le Cunff, an ex-Googler who now runs the neuroscience-based productivity school, Ness Labs.[71] How do you know if something is relevant? Relevant to what? If you're heading into a career change or hoping to accomplish something outside your established patterns, your moonshot goal may not be relevant to your current situation.

Le Cunff suggests a different backronym for creating goals that's more appropriate for something of moonshot scale: making a PACT. PACT stands for purposeful, actionable, continuous, and trackable.

"While a SMART goal focuses on the outcome, the PACT approach focuses on the output," Le Cunff said. "It's about continuous growth rather than the pursuit of a well-defined achievement."[72]

The first and perhaps most important component in a PACT is *purpose*. Feeling connected to your goal through a deep inner drive sustains motivation. Ascribing meaning to a goal means you will likely work harder and longer to achieve it, increasing your chances of success. For Sir Dyson, the exciting possibility of creating cyclone vacuum technology gave him purpose. Purpose taps into intrinsic motivation, the internal driver for accomplishment, which research

---

71. Anne-Laure Le Cunff, "SMART Goals Are Not So Smart: Make a PACT Instead," *Ness Labs*, Ness Labs, July 13, 2020.
72. Ibid.

shows has longer-lasting positive effects on performance than extrinsic motivation, or outside influence.[73]

Actionable is also a more suitable replacement to the *achievable* metric in the SMART framework. Achievability is often nebulous, but actionable indicates that there are clear steps to take. While exponential success typically involves some amount of blind faith thinking, ("I don't know how we'll do it, but we'll get there"), actionable focuses on laying the next brick in the road toward the goal. This action-based approach shifts thinking to an internal locus of control, the belief that one is in control of their own destiny rather than subject to the whims of fate. Feeling a semblance of control over outcomes is mission-critical to goals, large or small. While the ultimate outcome may be out of your control (getting selected for the Olympic rowing team), the actions that can lead to it are within your control (getting up at five every morning to train). Breaking up larger goals into these smaller actions makes moonshots appear less daunting and helps the pursuer stay on track with the small steps to get there.

Continuity is the next critical component. Momentum is often overlooked but plays a significant role in long-term goals. Ever notice how the better you get at a certain skill, the more fun and exciting it is to practice? After the initial, fumbling few months of playing guitar, you'll get great joy and fulfillment in stringing together songs from chords you know by heart. Creating goals that involve *continuous* progress boosts a feeling of increased competence, which is one of the main ingredients in intrinsic motivation.

---

73. Anne-Laure Le Cunff, "Building Intrinsic Motivation," *Ness Labs*, Ness Labs, May 5, 2020.

The best way to foster momentum is to create systems and routines that are easily repeatable, said Le Cunff. Knowing where to pick up where you left off prevents choice paralysis, that dreaded forty minutes you spend browsing through Netflix trying to find the best option of what to watch. Choice paralysis has been modernized into the phrase FOBO, or Fear Of a Better Option.

FOBO and Choice Paralysis

If some is good, more must be better. This is a convenient little lie we tell ourselves as we sit on the couch with a full tub of ice cream and a spoon, in lieu of scooping ourselves a regular portion into a bowl. Thirty minutes later, bellies protruding and testing the limits of the elastic in our pants, we often find that more is not, indeed, always better.

Still, when it comes to choices, we tend to want as many options as possible. FOBO leaves us searching for all available possibilities, for fear we'll miss out. The thing is, we often end up in the terrible purgatory land of indecision.

Choice paralysis is epitomized by the famous jam experiment by psychologists Sheena Iyengar and Mark Lepper. In 2000, Iyengar and Lepper set up two tasting tables at an upscale supermarket in Menlo Park on different days.[74] On one day, the table had twenty-four varieties of jam for shoppers to sample and buy. On another day, Iyengar and Lepper displayed only six varieties of jam. Both days, shoppers were

---

74. Sheena S Iyengar and Mark R Lepper, "When Choice Is Demotivating: Can One Desire Too Much of a Good Thing," *Journal of Personality and Social Psychology*, January 2001, 995-1006.

encouraged to taste the jams and received a jam coupon if they did.[75]

The study revealed some surprising results. Though more people were drawn to the table with the larger variety of jams, the researchers found that shoppers were actually one-tenth as likely to buy from it as people who saw the small display. The paralysis of choice had left them deciding not to buy anything at all. Further investigation revealed something even more intriguing: Those who had purchased jam from the table of twenty-four options were less happy with their choice than those who had purchased from the table of six. FOBO, it seems, left people second-guessing their choice from the large spread. Those with blackberry jelly began to resent the fact they hadn't picked peach marmalade. Variety isn't always better.

To avoid this, we'll theoretically be better off saving our forty minutes of browsing in the Netflix vortex and watching *The Office* again, regardless of if we've seen the series ten times already. In the context of setting goals, removing the choice of which action to take helps set you on a continuous path. If you know you always lift weights on Tuesdays and go for runs on Thursdays, you've removed the inefficiency of choice and can better stick to your forward progress. Momentum starts to build. The final component in the PACT framework, trackable, ensures you are holding yourself accountable for the progress you make.

Setting a goal and building momentum are important defenses against one thing that kills moonshot goals like no other: fear.

---

75. Barry Schwartz, "More Isn't Always Better," *Harvard Business Review*, Harvard Business Publishing, August 1, 2014.

Facing Fear

Fear is like one of those terrible wheel clamps placed on a car tire to keep you from going anywhere after your fifth parking ticket this month. You can kick it and pout all you want, but in the event you want your car to do car things again, you have to face it head-on.

No one likes facing fear, so we often do some creative intellectual gymnastics to avoid it. Many people adopt stories like "I've always been this way, and so I'll always be this way," or, "I tried to become unafraid, and it didn't work, so why bother" and they live their *whole lives* with a tire boot on their car, straining their relationships by bumming rides or slowing their forward progress by walking every day. If that works for you, keep doing it. But I can promise that you won't find exponential success.

Fears rise up in crucial moments of life, and they can easily turn your moment of impact, that pivotal point where the exponential graph begins to curve up and to the right, into a fumbled opportunity. These are the moments when the free-thrower chokes, when the lecturer freezes up, when the actress panics and forgets her lines. Now, you have only one way out of this fear-driven trap: facing the darn thing.

But what if you could delegate the dragon-slaying duties of fear-facing to your superhero of choice? What if someone else could take over your body for the day and give the speech, run the race, shoot the shot for you? This just might be possible.

We'll start with a story. Once upon a time, a singer had terrible stage fright. Though she was incredibly talented, she would vomit before shows, panic in the dressing rooms, and was even known to flee out of fire exits from time to time to avoid putting on a performance.[76]

Her fears deeply affected her career, causing her to dread going on tour. Though her abilities were prodigious and her fame was growing, she'd get incredibly nervous before meeting other famous people. Eventually, she had the opportunity to meet one of her musical idols, Beyoncé. Moments before the meeting, our heroine had a full-blown anxiety attack. She pulled herself together enough for the quick hello but ran out to the balcony moments after it ended, bursting into tears.

On the balcony, she cried out to Beyoncé's famous alter ego. "What would Sasha Fierce do?" she sobbed. A lightbulb went off in her head. If her hero had an alter ego, why couldn't she? At that moment, she crafted up the alter ego Sasha Carter, a composite name of (fake) Sasha Fierce and (real) country music singer June Carter.[77]

Sasha Carter has gone on to become one of the world's best-selling and most celebrated artists, with millions of records sold, countless Grammys won, and a couple of Artist of the Year titles under her belt. Of course, no one knows that Sasha Carter is behind all of the success, her confident personality overcoming fear to handle all of the singing and dancing and performing. In fact, hardly anyone knows Sasha Carter exists at all. We know her simply as her real name, Adele.

Adele and Beyoncé are not the only successful people known for adopting alter egos to help them conquer their fear. In fact, an astounding number of high-caliber people use this technique to bypass unhelpful emotions and slip on a golden crown of confidence to maximize their full potential.

---

76. Touré, "Adele Opens Up about Her Inspirations, Looks, and Stage Fright," *Rolling Stone*, Rolling Stone, June 25, 2018.
77. Ibid.

Performance coach Todd Herman has spent twenty years coaching Olympic athletes, leaders, and entrepreneurs in how to adopt alter egos to unlock potential, a concept he wrote about in his book, *The Alter Ego Effect*.[78] The idea for using mental superheroes as a technique came to Herman after he met professional athlete Bo Jackson. Jackson confided in Herman that ever since he was a kid, he had mentally impersonated the cold, calculating, hockey-mask-wearing character Jason from the movie *Friday the 13th* when competing in sports.

Alter egos give the mind a tool to self-distance, says Rachel White, assistant professor of psychology at Hamilton College.[79] They allow the brain to take a step back from the situation and observe the whole picture more rationally. This, in turn, decreases feelings of anxiety and increases the perception of being in control.

Mentally removing ourselves from situations can help us tackle America's number one fear: public speaking. In a study at the University of Michigan, participants were told they were going to give a small speech. Half of the participants were asked to imagine themselves giving the talk from their own perspective while the other half was asked to picture it from a third-person point of view.[80]

The researchers recorded the two groups' pre-speech emotions and also measured their heart rate and blood pressure. People in the second group reported feeling less anxious and more optimistic before going into the presentation than the first group. The group who had mentally distanced

---

78. Todd Herman, *The Alter Ego Effect: The Power of Secret Identities to Transform Your Life*, 2, (New York: Harper Collins Publishers), 2019.

79. David Robson, "The 'Batman Effect': How Having an Alter Ego Empowers You," *The Life Project*, BBC, August 17, 2020.

80. Ibid.

themselves from the upcoming talk were also shown to be less physically agitated.

After the presentations, independent observers found that the mentally distanced group gave higher quality performances than the comparison group. Alter egos are an effective way of creating this mental distance. Whether Sasha Carter or Jason from *Friday the 13th* resonates with you, these silent superheroes can be a powerful weapon to bring to the battle of fear.

Stories

The reason alter egos are so powerful is because our lives are ruled by stories. Stories dictate how we make sense of the world, how we communicate with others, and how we view ourselves.

They are also one of the core principles of our humanness. Our ability to tell stories may be one of the most important factors that sets us apart from the animal kingdom, and one that has led to the exponential success of humans as a whole. As *Sapiens* author Yuval Noah Harari put it:

> *Homo sapiens* conquered this planet thanks above all to the unique human ability to create and spread fictions. We are the only mammals that can cooperate with numerous strangers because only we can invent fictional stories, spread them around, and convince millions of others to believe in them. As long as everybody believes in the same fictions, we all obey the same laws, and can thereby cooperate effectively.[81]

---

81. Yuval Noah Harari, "Yuval Noah Harari Extract: 'Humans Have Always Lived in the Age of Post-Truth. We're a Post-Truth Species.'" *The Guardian*, Guardian News and Media, August 5, 2018.

If, like Bo Jackson, we make ourselves believe the story that we are ruthless and undaunted on the playing field, that is what we become.

An important step in chasing a moonshot goal is crafting a narrative story around our identity in relation to our goals. When *Grit* author Angela Duckworth gave a talk at Google, she explained her theory of why Google employees call themselves "Googlers."[82] According to Duckworth's research, Google's employee nomenclature was probably a highly intentional, if not strategic, choice. In other groups she had studied, she noticed the same naming pattern emerge. West Point Military Academy cadets called themselves West Pointers. KIPP school students called themselves KIPPsters. Most of us have been a proud Tiger, Hawk, or Bulldog, per our school's mascot name. In each instance, the group name reflects a cohesive sense of shared identity and belonging. People are proud to be a part of a tribe.

"When people have a really strong cultural identity, they're usually able to express that as a noun," Duckworth said. According to Duckworth, this kind of tribalism and storytelling may make people grittier and more resilient at work.

The stories we tell may also predict our successes. Evidence of this is found in one area of our life you may not expect: romantic relationships. In one experiment, scientists conducted a longitudinal study on couples. They sat down with married couples who reported high satisfaction in their marriages and had them give an oral history of their relationship. Couples told their stories of how they met, what their weddings we like, and what the first year of marriage was

---

82. *Talks at Google*, "Grit: The Power of Passion and Perseverance | Angela Duckworth | Talks at Google," May 6, 2016, video, 51:59.

like. After the interviews, the researchers scored the stories on traits like fondness, affection, negativity toward spouse, and conflict resolution. Then they made predictions about the future of the relationships. Would the couple stay happily married? Would they divorce?[83]

Years later, the researchers followed up with the couples. Their hypotheses turned out to be eerily correct. With 93.6 percent accuracy, the researchers had predicted who would stay together and who would get divorced.

The study strongly indicated that how a couple told the story of their past was highly correlated with their future marital success. The stories we tell, mentally or outwardly, can have profound impacts on our outcomes.

Ben Horowitz, co-founder of Andreeson Horowitz, wrote a book on company culture called *What You Do Is Who You Are*.[84] The prequel to this book, focused on personal achievement, perhaps could have been called *What You Tell Yourself Is What You Do*. The stories we form in our minds dictate our actions, both consciously and subconsciously.

If you're really hungry and someone offers you a hamburger, chances are, you'll say yes. But if your personal story, your identity, is that you're a vegetarian, you'll decline without even thinking about it. The same works for moonshots. Whether you've written a successful book or not, telling yourself "I am an author" can help you sit down each day and do the work. Believing that "I am the fastest swimmer here," "I will cure cancer," or "I will get a part in this Broadway

83. Kim T. Buehlman, John M. Gottman, and Lynn F. Katz. "How a Couple Views Their Past Predicts Their Future: Predicting Divorce from an Oral History Interview." *Journal of Family Psychology* 5, no. 3-4 (1992): 295-318.

84. Ben Horowitz, "What You Do Is Who You Are," Andreessen Horowitz, accessed February 10, 2021.

musical," increases your resiliency to keep moving forward until your story becomes fact. This is likely why some people swear by manifestation journals or practices. As Angela Duckworth said, these narratives make us grittier.

Is there a catch? Well, yes. Of course. There aren't any hacks to exponential success, only pathways. The first catch is that you have to actually believe your story. You can't just say it, or it will lose meaning to you and fade away. Your moonshot has to be baked into your personal identity, inseparable from who you are as a person. The world will test your conviction unrelentingly. You must be committed to it without a doubt in your mind.

The second catch is that, if you are just starting out, your identity may have already been crafted by something negative. Internal monologues like "I always fail" and "I'm not good enough" are proverbial icebergs to your Titanic. The only way out of this trap is through action. "New identities require new evidence," James Clear writes in *Atomic Habits*.[85] To get out of this negative loop, you must choose a new goal and prove it to yourself with small wins. By writing a few hundred words a day, swimming extra laps, or auditioning for every musical that comes along, you can prove to yourself over time that you are who you want to be.

The stories we craft in our own minds are undoubtedly Archimedes levers; you just have to make sure the lever is lifting you in the direction you want to go. The final catch to using stories is in your moonshot goal itself.

---

85. James Clear, *Atomic Habits: An Easy & Proven Way to Build Good Habits & Break Bad Ones*, (New York: Random House, 2018), 58.

Absolute vs. Relative Goals

You can optimize for the perfect goal framework, adopt an alter ego, and tell yourself a story of success to get you well on your way toward achieving your moonshot. But, at the end of the day, how do you know if the goal you've selected is even a good one? One way to find out is a goal audit.

Oftentimes, goals are crafted to reflect what our peers want or what we think society wants of us, rather than what we truly want to accomplish. Because the motivation for these kinds of goals is extrinsic, chasing after and even achieving these goals can feel hollow and unfulfilling. Though humans are surprisingly skilled at hiding their true hopes and dreams while they chase external validation, our true intrinsic goals eventually break through the surface.

Brian Timar, a software engineer at SpaceX, recalls his realization that he perhaps wasn't pursuing a graduate degree in physics for the right reasons:

> One afternoon, while moving out of an apartment, I came across a cardboard box packed with binders and paper folders, full of notes accumulated over the past year. As I let it fall in front of the door, a thought dropped into my head and stuck there: None of this means anything to me. This was, nominally, the fruit borne of a year of my life, and it felt so viscerally wasted. Despair bought me honesty; by enrolling in graduate school, I'd made myself miserable for no reason. Why had I spent so much time in purposeless hard work? I arrived at a simple mechanism: an

excessive sensitivity to the desires of others, and a competitive environment.[86]

With some self-reflection, Timar began to metabolize how his goal had shifted over time. While at first he had taken interest in the subject of physics itself, his desire to excel in relation to others soon became his main obsession. His ambition soon focused on acquiring social capital as a result of his achievements. Eventually, he realized that what he thought was his dream felt both hollow and absurd.

Timar had fallen into a mimetic trap: the desire to imitate others and the inability to exit at the top, something not uncommon in academia. "It hurts to leave, and there's nowhere to go. It decouples the social reward signal from the rest of objective reality. You can spend years ascending ranks in a hierarchy without producing anything that the rest of humanity finds valuable," Timar said.[87]

This kind of mimetic trap is a frequently cited experience among young people in the Asian American community. In an episode of his Netflix show, *Patriot Act*, comedian Hasan Minhaj recounts the pressure put on Asian students by their parents. "Asians, just so you know, we are only 5.8 percent of the population but last year we were 22.2 percent of Harvard's admitted class," he says. "We are straight dunking on every other minority group, but in classic Asian parent fashion, we're like, 22 percent? Why not 100 percent?"[88]

Minhaj has experienced this same kind of relative and extrinsic goal setting by his own parents. Though he has

---

86. Brian Timar, "Mimetic Traps," *Brian Timar* (blog), updated May 19, 2019.
87. Ibid.
88. "Hasan Minhaj Didn't Become a Lawyer," *NPR*, NPR, updated November 14, 2018.

hosted the White House Correspondents' Dinner and has been named one of *Time* magazine's 100 Most Influential People, Minhaj says his father still reminds him that if things don't work out, he can still save up for law school.[89, 90] Luckily, Minhaj followed his intrinsic goal of pursuing comedy, which continues to launch him forward in a wildly successful career.

For Brian Timar, the big mistake had been focusing on a relative goal, beating his peers, rather than an absolute goal, learning how the world works. While both are motivating, relative goals eventually feel unrewarding and futile. When Timar figured out he wasn't telling a true story to himself, he ended up leaving grad school and vowing to himself not to fall into this kind of trap again.

A good policy for avoiding relative goals and pursuing absolute goals is asking yourself why something matters to you. If the answer comes easily, you're probably on the right track. If not, you may want to reevaluate.

Absolute goals can seem daunting, particularly when they are on a moonshot scale. But chasing them is both exciting and energizing, conducive of a collaborative, rather than jealous, attitude. Those who adopt absolute, intrinsically motivated goals that align with their identities are more likely to stick with them in the long term. These goals won't change as their peer group fluctuates, and they don't require competition to pursue. People pursuing these goals enjoy the journey. They find fulfilment that carries them through the rough spots and play their own game long enough to enjoy the successes that come with perseverance.

89. Trevor Noah, "Hasan Minhaj," Pioneers, *TIME*, accessed February 10, 2021.
90. "Hasan," *NPR*.

In the end, exponential success requires setting a goal. Choosing an absolute goal based on intrinsic motivation and linked to your personal story is a great place to start. Framing it with a PACT and using techniques like alter egos to combat fear help keep you on track. Armed with this toolkit, you'll still probably try and fail five thousand times, just like Sir Dyson. But success awaits those who work for it.

CHAPTER 5

BIG FISH, SMALL POND

―――――

Build something 100 people love, not something
1 million people kind of like.

—BRIAN CHESKY

Minimum Viable Opus

You've picked your big, hairy, audacious goal. You have your
moonshot on the mind. Now, how do you even get started?
Most creators start with an MVP, a minimum viable
product. An MVP is the smallest, most basic working version
of the ultimate dream you have in mind. Jeff Bezos started
Amazon with a bare-bones website and shipping operation
that he ran out of his garage. Brian Chesky and Joe Gebbia
first rented out an air mattress in their San Francisco loft
apartment on their journey to creating Airbnb.[91]

---

91. Avery Hartmans, "'Amazon' Wasn't the Original Name of Jeff Bezos'
Company, and 14 Other Little-Known Facts about the Early Days of
Amazon," *Business Insider*, Business Insider, February 3, 2021.

The purpose of an MVP is to try something out at a low cost and iterate until it becomes the best version possible. Minimum viable product creation is a keystone of the lean startup methodology, an alternative to the traditional entrepreneurship model. The methodology was based on the work of Steve Blank, a Stanford entrepreneurship professor who saw glaring flaws in conventional models of entrepreneurship. The old way of doing things was broken, Blank believed. He writes:

> According to the decades-old formula, you write a business plan, pitch it to investors, assemble a team, introduce a product, and start selling as hard as you can. And somewhere in this sequence of events, you'll probably suffer a fatal setback. The odds are not with you: As new research by Harvard Business School's Shikhar Ghosh shows, 75 percent of all startups fail.[92]

By using MVPs, the lean approach reduces these barriers and allows founders to bring products to market faster and more effectively than the old approach. It's also a great way to get started on creating your moonshot.

You probably know the term *magnum opus*, "great work" in Latin. The subtext left out of this concept is that no piece of work is great in the beginning. Even if you would love to book an Airbnb in Turks and Caicos right now, you probably wouldn't have enjoyed staying on Chesky and Gebbia's air mattress when the business was in its infancy. The first versions of things are almost always crude; just ask parents who have given their kid a violin for the first time.

---

92. Steve Blank, "Why the Lean Start-Up Changes Everything," *Entrepreneurship, Harvard Business Review*, updated February 9, 2018.

LinkedIn cofounder Reid Hoffman said, "If you are not embarrassed by the first version of your product, you've launched too late."[93] The most important step is to put something out in the world, the MVP version of your eventual *opus*, and start working on your craft. Next, take what's ugly and make it better. You can't improve on something that never exists, but you can take something small and bad and build off of it. If people hate it, they'll probably tell you, and you can use their feedback to your advantage.

Feedback, in fact, is such a big part of the entrepreneurship world that many startups are now choosing to "build in public," that is, to allow the public to witness their whole process of developing and releasing new products.[94] Not only do these companies get instant and frequent feedback, but they also show the transparency and authenticity that consumers crave. This is in contrast to the *stealth* methodology, where companies build and recruit in secret without releasing any information on their proprietary offerings for sometimes years, attempting to keep the curtain closed to dissuade competitors. This technique works for companies who want to polish their offering and protect it from the public eye until it's ready, but it can also fall flat. "Godspeed to the startups building in 'stealth mode,' but they often exit their silence period only to find out nobody cared and they're two years behind on marketing," said startup founder and VC partner at FirstMark, Matt Turck.[95]

93. Nick Saint, "If You're Not Embarrassed by the First Version of Your Product, You've Launched Too Late," *Business Insider*. Business Insider, updated November 13, 2009.
94. Milan Kordestani, "Building in Public: How Tech Companies Master Product-Market Fit," *Entrepreneur*, Entrepreneur Media, updated November 13, 2020.
95. Matt Turck (@mattturck), Twitter, February 22, 2021, 11:14 a.m.

No matter what your moonshot goal is, you likely want to start with a *minimum viable opus*, the smallest possible working version of your end project. This may be a basic blog before writing your first book or building a model helicopter before inventing the electric helicopter. Like the tax collector in *Stranger Than Fiction* who finally buys himself an electric guitar, if you want to chase your dream, you just have to dive in and start.

Big Fish, Small Pond

While you begin building your minimum viable opus, you'll want to start thinking about who will interact with it.

One of the first questions a venture capitalist will ask about a potential startup investment is: "Is there product-market fit?" Anyone who wants to sell something needs to make sure it's a good match for their audience. You wouldn't want to advertise cat food to eight-year-olds, for example, or Super Soaker water blasters to seventy-year-old cat ladies. There's no product-market fit.

A variation of this question is relevant for exponential success. In chasing this goal, one must ask: How well does my relative environment support my success? Research indicates that, at least in the beginning of your journey, it pays to be a big fish in a small pond.

In 2018, a Stanford-led research team set out to study students whose abilities were a mismatch for their relative environment.[96] In particular, they evaluated high-performing

96. Krysten Crawford, "Stanford Education Study Provides New Evidence of 'Big-Fish-Little-Pond' Effect on Students Globally," *Research Stories*, Stanford University, last modified December 13, 2018.

eighth graders in low-ranked schools and underperformers at highly ranked schools. They wanted to know if high achievers did better or worse in challenging environments and what kind of emotional toll relative environments took on the students. The researchers evaluated nearly two hundred thousand students in over thirty countries and regions, looking at test scores as well as measures of academic self-concept.

A surprising pattern emerged. High-achieving students fared better emotionally in lower-achieving schools.[97] The results remained consistent across genders, countries, income levels, and through all different subjects of study—math to science to history. This data went against conventional wisdom. Don't we thrive on challenge and learning that keeps pace with our abilities? Aren't students supposed to be academically stimulated?

The study measured the emotional metric of academic self-concept, or how capable a student believes they are. More than just basic confidence, academic self-concept is an incredibly important factor in student outcomes. Studies show it affects student performance and attitudes in the classroom as well as their chances of advancing to more rigorous programs.[98]

The researchers noticed that, in high-achieving schools, students compared themselves to their equally high-achieving peers and lost confidence in their own abilities. Conversely, high-achievers who found themselves easily at the top of the pack in lower-achieving schools maintained strong confidence in their abilities. "We have a tendency to compare ourselves to others in terms of our abilities and, because of

---

97. Ibid.
98. Ibid.

that, we tend to feel better or worse about ourselves. It is fundamental to who we are," said the lead researcher, Dr. Prashant Loyalka.[99]

It has long been speculated that being a big fish in a small pond was advantageous, but this study confirmed that carefully choosing environments can have a big impact on one's chances of success.

Of course, this principle must be used with moderation. It's no secret that "gifted and talented" high school students who go on to highly-competitive schools like the Ivy Leagues often experience a rude awakening during their first year. Not being the smartest one in the room for the first time can deflate a fragile ego, leaving high-achievers feeling lost and defeated. Still, you wouldn't want to intentionally seek out understimulating people and environments. Surrounding oneself with smart and driven individuals is a cornerstone component of success, and the benefits of selecting a competitive environment can far outweigh the negatives.

What, then, makes the difference between an environment with too much challenge and an environment with too little? The answer may lie in the size. Starting out in a small pond is perhaps the perfect way to develop before graduating to the ocean.

Beginning with a niche audience or subject of expertise can expedite impact and success. PayPal founder-turned-billionaire-investor Peter Thiel advises entrepreneurs to focus on a very niche target audience in the beginning. In *Zero to One*, he writes: "Always err on the side of starting too small. The reason is simple: it's easier to dominate a small market

---

99. Ibid.

than a large one. If you think your initial market might be too big, it almost certainly is."[100]

Thiel discusses how Mark Zuckerberg didn't try and capture the billion people who currently use Facebook—he designed a website specifically for the students at his university. Likewise, eBay targeted niche, hobbyist sellers like Beanie Baby fanatics for years before growing to accommodate a wide range of products and audiences.[101] Whether you are writing content online, developing a new line of shampoos, or composing electronic dance music, there are several reasons that this niche-first approach is effective.

First, small markets are less likely to be targeted by a lot of companies or people. There will be less saturation in your market and therefore less competition. Second, it's much easier to customize and tweak your offering to suit your market to ensure it's a good fit before scaling too quickly. The better the product-market fit, the more loyal your followers or customers will be. Third, starting small allows you to fail fast with minimal consequences. If you're lucky, you'll have multiple opportunities to pivot before the ship sinks.

1,000 True Fans

Finding a niche market or endeavor perfect for your unique abilities may just be the critical stepping stone to exponential success, however, this advice may be counter-intuitive. Many people believe great creators need large audiences. There's a reason there's a whole section of the economy dedicated to

---

100. Peter Thiel, *Zero to One: Notes on Startups, or How to Build the Future*, (London: Virgin Books, 2014), 53.
101. Ibid.

mass publicity and gaining followers online. In 2019 alone, advertisers lost an estimated $1.3 billion marketing to fake followers on social media.[102] While enormous followings might be trendy, having a small market of dedicated, loyal supporters may be just as advantageous. In fact, you may only need a few hundred believers in your mission to have a successful career.

Kevin Kelly, senior founding editor of *Wired* magazine, believes creators only need about a thousand true fans to find success, an idea that has since made its rounds through creator communities of all varieties.

According to Kelly, a true fan is someone who loves your mission so much they will buy anything you make.[103] They are the enthusiastic fanatics who will brave a dive bar in Queens to see you play with your band, or who will give everyone they know a copy of your book for Christmas. A true fan will come to your yoga retreat in Panama or commission you annually to do a custom sculpture of their pug. You can count on these supporters to back you, whatever you create.

The math checks out. If you can make $100 a year from each of your fans, you only need a thousand of them to make six figures a year. This number can be adjusted depending on what you charge and how much money you need to live. If ten thousand people only like you a little bit and are willing to toss you $10 a year, or if you only need $80K to live and eighty people will spend $1,000 on your work each year, you've got it made.

---

102. Megan Cerullo, "Influencer Marketing Fraud Will Cost Brands $1.3 Billion in 2019," CBS News, CBS Interactive, updated July 25, 2019.

103. Kevin Kelly, "1,000 True Fans," *The Technium* (blog), last modified March 4, 2008.

You don't need to be the next Yo-Yo Ma or Simone Biles to acquire this modest level of support; reaching this goal is achievable with just about any half-baked idea or skill. My favorite new expression is: "The bar is on the floor," meaning the barrier to entry is incredibly low, and guess what? When it comes to finding success by building a modest audience, the bar is on the floor.

Kelly writes, "As far as I can tell there is nothing—no product, no idea, no desire—without a fan base on the internet. Everything made, or thought of, can interest at least one person in a million; it's a low bar."[104] The internet is a weird place. Whatever your niche, bizarre interest, or uncommon skill, it has a place for you. If you don't believe me, go spend some time on r/BreadStapledToTrees, where almost 300,000 Redditors discuss, and post pictures of, stapling slices of bread to trees.[105] (Environmental note: Participants are encouraged to remove the staples when they are done.)

The beauty of being a creator in the age of the internet is that you can find and connect with your fans, no matter how obscure your product. Of course, a thousand people is a rough estimate. Fifteenth-century Florentine artists really only needed one patron with deep pockets to make a living. If the end goal is the creation of something new and beautiful in the world, it shouldn't matter how many people actually celebrate and support it. Writer Seth Godin remarked, "You need to alter what you do and how you do it so that 1,000 true fans is sufficient to make you very happy."[106]

104. Ibid.
105. "r/BreadStapledToTrees," Reddit, accessed February 17, 2021.
106. Seth Godin, "Seth's Blog," Seth's Blog, last modified March 4, 2008.

I view the thousand true fans as a baseline. Hitting this number builds an Archimedes lever to exponential success by giving you enough cushion and financial backing to continue to do your work. Find happiness in this number, and you can live out your days contentedly underwater-basket-weaving in peace.

Consider, however, that for each *true fan* or *superfan*, you could have nineteen other fans who support you occasionally or even just once. Once you reach the one-thousand true fan mark, there will likely be twenty thousand people in the world who at least vaguely know who you are and like what you do. Now we're talking.

Twenty thousand people is an enormous network. The average number of LinkedIn connections a typical user has is four hundred, meaning by the time you reach your true fan baseline, you have fifty times the number of people available to support you than the average professional.[107]

Use this network wisely and you have all the tools for true exponential gains. Aiming to capture the hearts and minds of just a thousand people is a great way to start. As Kelly writes, "On your way, no matter how many fans you actually succeed in gaining, you'll be surrounded not by faddish infatuation, but by genuine and true appreciation. It's a much saner destiny to hope for. And you are much more likely to actually arrive there."[108]

---

107. Aatif Awan, "The Power of LinkedIn's 500 Million Member Community," *LinkedIn Official Blog*, last modified April 24, 2017.
108. Ibid.

Shrink the Pond

Reaching the thousand true fans mark requires capturing the minds and hearts of people outside your social circle. Your mom might be your number one fan no matter what you do. Your best friends might comprise your top five or ten fans, and your entire social circle could claim the top 150 spots, if you're lucky. Attracting complete strangers to your mission is a separate beast. The base requirement is that you must do something unique. Keep your day job if you want, but it's the rare working professional that achieves *exponential* success without some kind of side hustle or passion that sets them apart from the crowd.

Baseball analysis is how Nate Silver, founder of the polling aggregate website FiveThirtyEight, became the paragon of statistical forecasting in the US. Silver took some time to find his niche, though. After graduating college, Silver spent three and a half years working at one of the Big Four accounting organizations, a job he hated.[109] In his free time, he did something he loved: eclectic statistical analysis. And it involved a lot of beans and cheese.

In 2007, Silver moved to Wicker Park, Chicago, an area dotted with authentic little taquerias.[110] Ever on the quest to quantify the world, Silver decided to get to know his new neighborhood better by working on a unique side project. He started a website called the "Burrito Bracket" that pitted the best Mexican restaurants in the area against one another.

---

109. Stephen J. Dubner, "FREAK-Quently Asked Questions: Nate Silver," *Freakonomics*, Freakonomics, LLC, last modified March 12, 2009.

110. Nate Silver, "In Search of America's Best Burrito," *FiveThirtyEight*, FiveThirtyEight, updated June 5, 2014.

Each weekend, he'd go get a burrito from two of them to determine which restaurant would advance to the next round of the competition. He evaluated each establishment based on twelve different characteristics, including categories like texture, garnishes, and efficiency of service, and posted statistics of each of their chances of winning on his blog.[111]

Numerical analysis seemed to be his forte, and, after quitting his day job and doing a brief stint of online poker playing, Silver turned his talents in statistics to the world of baseball. Armed with a degree in economics from the University of Chicago and an uncanny ability for picking winners, Silver developed PECOTA, an algorithmic system for predicting Major League Baseball player performance. PECOTA was quickly snapped up by Baseball Prospectus, a baseball analysis company, with Silver leading the charge.[112] Silver's talent was in full swing.

By this point, Silver had made a name for himself. *New York Magazine* called him the Spreadsheet Psychic.[113] Flying under the radar, Silver decided to take on a pen name, perhaps inspired by his previous burrito endeavors. He called himself Poblano.

With the new nom de plume, Silver turned his talents anonymously to US election forecasting, He began aggregating polling data on his new website, FiveThirtyEight, and publishing his eerily correct predictions under his chili

111. Nate Silver, "El Taco Veloz [#2] Defeats Picante Taqueria [#10]," *The Burrito Bracket* (blog), last modified November 10, 2007.
112. Adam Sternbergh, "How Nate Silver Went From Forecasting Baseball Games to Forecasting Elections," *New York Magazine*, New York Magazine, last modified October 9, 2008.
113. Ibid.

pepper-inspired nickname.[114] The anonymous blogger was soon out-forecasting most major pollsters, causing quite a stir in the analytics community. Eventually, Silver revealed his true identity to the world. The baseball analytics nerd is now an award-winning statistician with six honorary doctorates and credentials at both *ESPN* and the *New York Times*. *Forbes* has called him "the world's most famous living statistician" and Freakonomics dubbed him "the biggest new political star after a certain family named Obama."[115, 116] Tens of millions of people visit his website for election predictions every presidential cycle.[117]

Silver could have stayed in his boring Chicago job. Instead, he started with a minimum viable opus and grew it into something huge. Though his Burrito Bracket days are over, Silver quickly garnered his first thousand true fans by taking his talents to unique new markets.

Shrinking your pond embraces the age-old Apple slogan: "Think Different." Going exponential means capitalizing on your unique strengths and finding out what you can do better in the world than almost everyone else. It means that even if you work a regular 9 to 5, you should always seek out outside opportunities and ways to differentiate yourself. Just as Silver followed his burrito-driven passion toward analytics and predictions, finding your niche specialty can help you identify a strategic small pond to pursue big dreams.

---

114. Andrew Romano, "Polling: Baseball's Stat Star on Campaign '08," *Newsweek*, Newsweek, last modified June 7, 2008.

115. Meta S. Brown, "Why Nate Silver's Forecasts Are Better Than Yours (And How You Can Improve)," *Forbes*, Forbes Magazine, last modified July 31, 2016.

116. Stephen J. Dubner, "FREAK-Quently Asked Questions: Nate Silver," *Freakonomics*, Freakonomics, LLC, last modified March 12, 2009.

117. "Fivethirtyeight.com Traffic Statistics," *SimilarWeb*, SimilarWeb LTD, accessed January 19, 2021.

CHAPTER 6

THE PARETO PRINCIPLE

Believe it or not, it is not only possible to accomplish
more by doing less, it is mandatory.

—TIM FERRISS

It is not shortage of time that should worry us, but
the tendency for the majority of time to be spent in
low-quality ways.

—RICHARD KOCH

Somewhere along your moonshot journey, you may wonder
if different actions produce results that are actually dramatically different. You may question if these Archimedes levers
to success even exist, or if some people just strike it lucky.

Certainly, luck plays a part in exponential success; we'll
get to that in chapter twelve. But there is also a hidden factor
that compounds almost all successful moonshot achievements: The Pareto Principle.

The Pareto Principle, also called the 80:20 rule, indicates that there is a predictable asymmetry of effort to outcome. In other words, levers are everywhere. You get to choose whether to sit on the see-saw opposite a pebble, a 20-pound dumbbell, or something even heavier. The principle has helped both individuals and creators maximize their abilities, potential, and profits for decades, and learning to harness it is a key force multiplier for exponential success.

The principle was discovered in the late 1800s by Italian economist Vilfredo Pareto when he noticed that 20 percent of the pea plants in his garden produced 80 percent of the peas.[118] Curious, he thought, that some of the plants were far and away more productive than others. Perhaps this unusual observation would have escaped his notice were it not for the fact that he had also been studying the relationship between population and wealth at that time in Europe. Astoundingly, Pareto noticed the same ratio in wealth distribution: In nearly every locale in England, 20 percent of the population reliably owned about 80 percent of the land. He reviewed historical land ownership data going back many years in the country and found the same pattern. To his amazement, the same 80:20 ratio emerged in data from other European countries as well.[119]

Pareto realized that a number of factors in nature assumed this asymmetrical, yet predictable, pattern. He knew the pattern couldn't be just an accident and indeed had significant implications. Marketing and public discourse

---

118. Mary Hall, "Real-Life Examples of the 80-20 Rule (Pareto Principle) in Practice," *Investopedia*, Investopedia, updated November 6, 2020.

119. Richard Koch, *The 80/20 Principle: The Secret of Achieving More with Less*, 3.1. Vol. 3.1. (New York, NY: Doubleday, 2008), 23.

weren't his strong suits, however, so the idea died out for about half a century.

The Pareto Principle lay mostly dormant until it was revived in the 1940s by management consultant Joseph M. Juran. Juran was the leader behind the quality control revolution in manufacturing. In his consulting work, Juran found that the 80:20 principle could be applied to many different elements of quality control in manufacturing.[120] In his book, the *Quality Control Handbook*, Juran extolled the benefits of the 80:20 rule, bringing it into the public consciousness. Juran dubbed the concept, "The Rule of the Vital Few." He demonstrated many times over that 20 percent of manufacturing mistakes caused 80 percent of the defects in products. He also found that 20 percent of the employees drove 80 percent of the businesses' success. Identifying the key 20 percent of factors, therefore, became a crucial task for any company who wished to succeed and an exceptional differentiator for companies that were chasing enormous, moonshot-level success.[121]

Though Juran focused his Rule of the Vital Few primarily on manufacturing, perhaps his greatest contribution to modern society was identifying the Pareto Principle's prevalence in an astounding range of contexts, from social and behavioral studies to nature and technology.

It wasn't long before the concept began to pick up speed. IBM latched onto the idea in the early 1960s, becoming one of the first big corporations to maximize the utility of the Pareto Principle. IBM engineers realized that their computers

---

120. Mark Best and Duncan Neuhauser, "Joseph Juran: Overcoming Resistance to Organizational Change," *Quality and Safety in Health Care* 15, no. 5 (October 1, 2006): 380-82.
121. Koch, *The 80/20 Principle*, 26.

spent 80 percent of their time processing about 20 percent of the code. With this knowledge, they immediately rewrote the software to make the most-used code more accessible and user friendly, placing them far ahead of their competition in terms of machine efficiency and speed.[122]

Identifying the high-impact code helped IBM maximize the important parts of the technology and brought compounding returns to the company.

In business, the Pareto Principle appears again and again, sometimes 82:18 or 75:25, but usually roughly in the same ballpark. As Richard Koch writes in his book, *The 80/20 Principle,* companies often find that 80 percent of the sales come from 20 percent of their client base. Similarly, 80 percent of profits tend to come from 20 percent of the work being done.[123]

The Pareto Principle extends far beyond just business, however. Back when video stores abounded, 20 percent of the tapes rented accounted for 80 percent of revenues.[124] People apparently just want to watch Tom Cruise movies and *The Hangover* multiple times in a row instead of branching into indie films. In health care, "high social cost" individuals, comprising 20 percent of the population, use 80 percent of the available health care resources.[125] Even birds follow the rule: 80 percent of birds seen in a particular area belong to 20 percent of the area's species.[126]

---

122. Ibid, 27.
123. Ibid, 20.
124. N. R. Kleinfeld, "A Tight Squeeze at Video Stores," *The New York Times,* May 1, 1988.
125. Nicola Davis, "High Social Cost Adults Can Be Predicted from as Young as Three, Says Study," *The Guardian,* December 12, 2016.
126. Fred J. Rispoli, et al., "Even Birds Follow Pareto's 80-20 Rule," *Significance* 11, no. 1 (February 2014): 37-38.

Pea plants to business to birds, what exactly causes the Pareto Principle? Is it a secret from the Illuminati, a sign of the devil, or a perfect ratio of nature?

Well, we know that it's not just an accident. "Probability theory tells us that it is virtually impossible for all the applications of the 80:20 Principle to occur randomly, as a freak of chance," Koch writes. The recurrence of the Pareto Principle suggests that it is, in fact, a power law, a functional relationship between two quantities. Power laws deal with exponents that respond to one another (remember $Y = MX + B$?) and have been used to describe everything from sizes of moon craters to city populations and frequency of words in any human language.[127]

Great, so how does this impact my own success?

The most important use-case for the Pareto Principle in success is understanding that 20 percent of your time, energy, and inputs (anything you consume, from media to food) create 80 percent of your outputs, which may or may not put you on a successful path. This relationship is not a little bit asymmetrical, it's wildly asymmetrical. People who achieve their moonshot goals, or *personal legends* as Paulo Coelho calls them in *The Alchemist*, know how to leverage the Pareto Principle to their advantage.[128]

Consider that 80 percent of your happiest moments come from 20 percent of your actions. Identifying the small proportion of inputs that result in the most happiness allows you to double-down on them.

---

127. M. E. J. Newman, "Power Laws, Pareto Distributions and Zipf's Law," Department of Physics and Center for the Study of Complex Systems University of Michigan, Ann Arbor, updated May 29, 2006.

128. Paulo Coelho and Alan Clarke, *The Alchemist*, New York, NY: HarperOne, 2018.

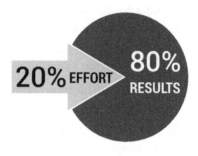

For example, perhaps you go for a run several times a week, attend a cooking class, and spend a few minutes each day playing with your dog. As far as you can tell, the combination of these three things produces the majority of your weekly joy. Turn an 80:20 lens on these activities, however, and you may discover some surprising results. Now that you think about it, your knees have been hurting every time you go for a run and sometimes stay sore for days afterward, leaving you grumpy and in pain. Traffic is always bad going to and from your cooking class, and you're always a little resentful about the cost of the class; $85 is a hefty price tag to cough up to make some simple pad thai.

Playing with Fido, however, leaves you rolling on the floor in a fit of endless giggles. Your smile is biggest when you're playing tug-of-war and throwing his tennis ball in the sunshine at the local dog park. Hours after playing with the dog, you're still more relaxed and content than before.

So where does the Pareto Principle come in? Well, if you guessed that playtime with Fido is your 20 percent ticket to 80 percent happiness, you're correct. Now you have action items to work from. You still want to run once in a while, but you add in a yoga class instead of running twice per week.

You quit the cooking class entirely and decide to just cook your friends nice meals once a month. You spend as much time as possible, up to several times a day now, laughing and playing with your dog. Happiness is at an all-time high. Applying the Pareto Principle mindset to all things in life—business, job, love, family, fun—gives you a framework for maximizing what's important.

The hardest part of applying this principle is that it doesn't immediately sound correct. Eighty percent of my income comes from twenty percent of my working hours? Are you sure? Eighty percent of my achievements come from twenty percent of my actions?

Yes, it's likely. But it can be quite difficult to grasp. As Koch writes:

> The reason that the 80:20 principle is so valuable is that it is counterintuitive. We tend to expect that all causes will have roughly the same significance. That all customers are equally valuable. That every bit of business, every product, and every dollar of sales revenue is as good as any other…
>
> We tend to assume that 50 percent of causes or inputs will account for 50 percent of results or outputs. There seems to be a natural, almost democratic, expectation that causes and results are generally equally balanced. And, of course, sometimes they are. But this "50/50 fallacy" is one of the most inaccurate and harmful, as well as the most deeply rooted, of our mental maps. The 80:20 Principle asserts that when two sets of data, relating to causes and results, can be examined and

analyzed, the most likely result is that there will be a pattern of imbalance.[129]

We like to see the world as an ordered, logical place. We strive to see equal and opposite reactions to every action. But the truth is, though there is order, there is also imbalance. The fortunate aspect is that, if we know how to recognize it, this imbalance works in our favor. Used properly, it's an Archimedes lever for exponential success.

Two clear implications come out of the Pareto Principle. First, it's imperative to maximize your 20 percent time. As with playing with Fido, the first step is identifying what your 20 percent best time is spent doing. If you're a writer, you may be surprised to discover that, while 10 percent of your most productive time is actually spent writing, the other 10 percent might be going for long walks and thinking, sourcing ideas for your next project. Action item: Go for more walks and/or walk for longer. Koch estimates that it is feasible to turn this 20 percent peak time into 40 percent in one year.[130]

The second action item is to decrease your 80 percent non-peak time. This time is generally bifurcated into two categories: obligations to other people and to *necessary evils*.

Obligations swallow up time like Takeru Kobayashi downs hotdogs. To start, be fiercely protective of your time, only saying yes to things you absolutely, critically want to do. Apply Derek Sivers' "If it's not a hell yeah, it's a no" framework.[131] Aggressively. For many people, this comes with the realization that they want to freelance or work for themselves.

---

129. Koch, *The 80/20 Principle*, 24.
130. Ibid.
131. Derek Sivers, "Hell Yeah Or No: What's Worth Doing," Derek Sivers, accessed March 6, 2021.

Being told where to be and what to do for 40 hours a week can quickly zap the joy and productivity out of even the most driven people. Even for those in more traditional workspaces, taking agency over their time and delegating where possible can free up countless hours and mind space. You don't have to go all *Four Hour Work Week*, but delegating, automating, and declining things will significantly increase your output time.

The second component to non-peak hours are the necessary evils. Necessary evils are things like chores and must-dos and the occasional horrible experience like going to the DMV. Some of these can't be escaped and some can. The best thing to do for these is eliminate them if possible and make them more pleasant if you can't.

Manhattanites are experts at this, I learned the summer I lived in New York City. It was only after standing in a forty-five-minute line in a two-story Trader Joe's near Union Square that I realized why most city goers eat takeout almost every night. The whole shopping, cooking, and cleaning process can be an enormous time-suck, particularly in the city where you have to take a whole carnival of subways and elevators and grocery-cart-escalators just to complete the ordeal. At the time, I was broke and couldn't afford to eat out often, so I eventually learned to pop in a great podcast or audiobook during the whole experience, doubling my enjoyment factor. Still, I learned how to avoid peak times and shop at small neighborhood bodegas instead of braving the crowds.

New Yorkers also get their laundry picked up and delivered. I first regarded this as an incredibly pompous endeavor until the third time I rode the elevator down from the fourteenth floor in my building in a single morning with a full basket of laundry only to discover every one of the washers was still in use. Again, I was broke and couldn't afford to get my laundry done, but I stopped resenting my friends who did it.

The great lesson of the Pareto Principle is that you must maximize the upside (which can be hard to identify) and minimize the downside (which is much larger than you think). This all jumps into great clarity when you realize what the opposite of the principle means. If 20 percent of your actions produce 80 percent of your successes, 80 percent of your actions produce only 20 percent. That means you are largely wasting your time, four-fifths of the time. Juran referred to the 20 percent as "the vital few" and to the 80 percent as "the trivial many."[132]

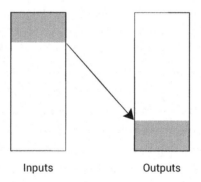

Inputs   Outputs

The Pareto Principle suggests that you should go deep on a few, carefully selected things rather than broad on lots of things. The best trick to identify which areas to maximize is figuring out where you already have an edge. Everyone is significantly better at one or a few things than most other people. Perhaps you have an *uncanny* ability to do voice impressions of certain political figures. You might double-down

132. Koch, *The 80/20 Principle*, 26.

and become the next Alec Baldwin on *Saturday Night Live*. Maybe you have a steady hand and are a particularly gifted writer; you could become the next Atul Gawande, a surgeon and bestselling author.

The power law of the Pareto Principle will either work for or against you. Taking the time to identify and maximize the upside produces compounding returns in the long run.

Whatever your talents, capitalize on the things you have a slight edge in doing, identify the 20 percent of your actions and time that increase that particular skill, and milk that 20 percent for all it's worth.

CHAPTER 7

IN FLOW

———

> There's this focus that, once it becomes intense, leads to a sense of ecstasy, a sense of clarity: you know exactly what you want to do from one moment to the other.
>
> —MIHALY CSIKSZENTMIHALYI

The Power of the F-Word

As the offspring of two former ski bums in Montana, I grew up scrambling around in the wilderness. At some point, my parents and brother and I all got into rock climbing. Granted, at ten years old, my main motivation was actually more focused on eating snacks and reading books in the shade while other people climbed than actually scaling rocks. For the most part during these outdoor excursions, I largely tuned out the family activity—Dad coiling rope and sorting through gear, our golden retriever Misty trying to eat whoever's sandwich was left unattended.

There was a certain moment on those outings, however, where everyone paid attention. These moments occurred when my mom, courageous but a little scared, would hit a challenging section on the wall and get stuck. She would try and fall, working and reworking the moves and trusting her harness to catch her with each failed attempt. Eventually, she'd get frustrated enough to announce it was time for her *magic words*. We held our collective breath. This is what we'd been waiting for.

In a burst of energy, a string of expletives would pour from her mouth as she somehow channeled both the tongue and physique of a sailor and launched herself up the wall. My dad, brother, and I would cheer and holler as she triumphantly summited whatever ledge had been holding her back.

Mom's magic words were actually rather effective. Studies have shown that saying expletives increases pain tolerance, after all.[133] She used the F-word in moments of maximum effort and only as a final resort. For her and everyone watching, these tense seconds were both stressful and powerful. Her F-word worked wonders.

Years later, once I got more serious about rock climbing, I discovered an even more powerful F-word: flow.

Rock climbing requires a perfect cocktail of focus. The risk of falling keeps the brain razor-sharp while the physical exertion channels energy and determination. The key to rock climbing, I learned, is entering a particular state of mind, an unbroken, ultra-focused, powerful channel of human attention and energy. With this mindset, which many people call flow state, even a novice climber can overcome both fear and physical obstacles to achieve incredible feats on the wall.

---

133. "Swearing Can Actually Increase Pain Tolerance," *ScienceDaily*, Science-Daily, updated July 13, 2009.

More than almost any other sport I have tried, rock climbing allows me to tune out the world completely, entering a state of flow. During these fleeting moments, everything melts away except the sound of my breath and body on the wall.

In Flow

As it turns out, entering flow is a powerful Archimedes lever for success in more than just athletic pursuits.

Flow state creates the most potent manifestation of creativity and productivity available to humans. Like paragliders tapping into thermal updrafts, regular flow state psychonauts are elevated toward their moonshot goals at an accelerated pace. Beyond just unbroken concentration, the mental state of flow affords people the opportunity to tap into almost supernatural abilities.

Toeing the line between challenge and mastery, flow occurs in moments of maximum energy output. Athletes and artists are known to sink into a flow state in moments of peak performance, where time seems to move differently. "In a state of flow, you're neither bored nor anxious, and you don't question your own adequacy. Hours pass without your noticing," author Susan Cain writes in *Quiet*.[134]

The Jedi Master of flow is revered Hungarian-American psychologist Mihaly Csikszentmihalyi (Me-High Cheek-Sent-Me-High), who discovered it around 1975 while he was on a mission to uncover the roots of happiness.

---

134. Susan Cain, *Quiet: The Power of Introverts in a World That Can't Stop Talking*, (New York: Random House, 2012) 81.

Csikszentmihalyi left WWII-battered Europe to study psychology in the US, and, having seen how many people were struggling with happiness after the war, he wanted to understand which conditions made people feel the most fulfilled.[135] During his research, Csikszentmihalyi discovered that people comfortably above the poverty line experienced about the same amount of happiness as the ultrawealthy. Class wasn't a proxy for happiness. Since the fulfilment baseline was relatively universal, Csikszentmihalyi set out to find exactly which moments made regular people feel *most* alive. He began by interviewing artists and scientists who loved their work. He found that, on their most productive days, these creative types entered almost a drug-induced state. One person he studied was a top American composer who regularly dipped into the state. Just the opposite of my experience in flow on the climbing wall, the composer lost all mental connection with his physical body. "His body disappears, his identity disappears from his consciousness, because he doesn't have enough attention, like none of us do, to really do well something that requires a lot of concentration, and at the same time to feel that he exists," Csikszentmihalyi said during a TED talk.[136] This state was flow state. It was beautiful, powerful, and hard to pin down. What conditions create it, Csikszentmihalyi wondered, and how can people step into it more easily?

After interviewing over eight thousand people from around the world, Csikszentmihalyi identified a "goldilocks zone" between skill and challenge where flow occurs. People must be skilled enough to feel competent in their work but

---

135. Csikszentmihalyi, "Flow," 2004.
136. Ibid.

challenged enough to stay focused and engaged. A novice tennis player playing against a professional is unlikely to enter flow; the difficulty would be too great. Conversely, the professional playing against a novice is unlikely to feel challenged enough to use their skills to their full potential. My mom was probably not experiencing flow when she used her magic words; the difficulty level was just a bit too high. Finding the sweet spot ensures someone is exerting their skills to their greatest ability while staying engaged and vigilant.

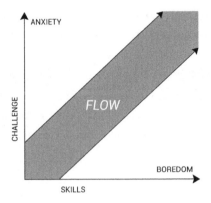

Flow requires such intense focus that the anxieties of the world disappear. Research shows that both the breath and the heart rate slow down in flow.[137] Bodily needs like hunger and tiredness slip from the mind and one is completely engaged in the task at hand.

Because some measure of skill or talent is required, it's challenging to enter flow when engaging in a completely new task. It's also almost impossible to enter it during an entirely

---

137. Örjan de Manzano, et al., "The Psychophysiology of Flow during Piano Playing," *Emotion* 10, no. 3 (June 2010), 301–11.

mundane activity. Though you might daydream while vacuuming the house, you aren't channeling the adrenaline and ferocity of focus needed for flow. If you are, I want to know where you're getting your vacuums. Some amount of difficulty in the task is necessary, but interestingly, the opposite of flow isn't discouragement, it's apathy. The largest single contributor to apathy is watching television, Csikszentmihalyi believes.[138]

Though they share similarities, flow is also different from hyper focus, which may occur during video game play or test taking. While hyper focus contains some negative characteristics like stress and overexertion, flow is inherently positive and is often associated with states of ecstasy.

Beyond just being a nice mental high, however, flow can have real implications on your chances of success. Flow state is correlated with subjective well-being, happiness, and life satisfaction, but also with increased performance and higher motivation.[139]

Flow as a Force Multiplier

Flexing your flow muscle regularly is imperative. Flow state isn't just a nice little boost, like a cup of coffee or a bump of white gold; it has been shown to increase productivity, creativity, and skill acquisition several hundred times more than the baseline.

---

138. Csikszentmihalyi, "Flow," 2004.
139. Mark Kasa and Zaiton Hassan, "Antecedent and Consequences of Flow: Lessons for Developing Human Resources," (*Procedia—Social and Behavioral Sciences* 97, 2013), 209-13.

A ten-year study at McKinsey & Co found that executives were five times more productive on average in a flow-like state.[140] That's an increase of 500 percent from the baseline. In theory, if an executive spent all of Monday in flow, they could accomplish every task for the entire workweek. By using the Pareto Principle to identify your 20 percent most powerful outputs, you can target flow state during these activities and maximize your producing ability exponentially more.

Harnessing flow is one of the most powerful force multipliers available to the human brain. The great thing about it is it's infinite, not finite. Instead of draining a person's abilities, flow has been shown to be so motivating, it's almost addictive.

So, how do we get into it? Flow is often described as a spontaneous state that arrives outside of one's control, much like the arrival of the creative Muse that Steven Pressfield describes in *The War of Art*. You prepare, you sit, you do the work, and you hope it arrives.

There are, however, several methodologies for inducing the state on demand. Steven Kotler, a leading expert on human performance, has studied and practiced flow state for the majority of his career.[141] Kotler, author of nine best-selling books and executive director of the Flow Research Collective, described two different hacks for entering flow state at will to podcaster Joe Rogan.[142]

Kotler's favorite way of inducing flow begins by going on a twenty-minute hike with his dogs. This creates

140. Susie Cranston and Scott Keller, "Increasing the 'Meaning Quotient' of Work," *McKinsey & Company*, McKinsey & Company, updated January 1, 2013.

141. "About Steven Kotler: High Performance Expert," Steven Kotler: Author and Speaker, accessed February 13, 2021.

142. Steven Kotler, interview with Joe Rogan, "#873 Steven Kotler," *The Joe Rogan Experience*, Spotify, updated November 17, 2016.

"exercise-induced transient hypofrontality," a fancy way of describing a calm brain state. Next, Kotler sprints uphill for five to seven minutes, boosting the endorphins in his system and energizing his body. Finally, Kotler runs down a steep cliff, introducing the feeling of risk and danger that produces the neurotransmitter norepinephrine and mandates complete brain clarity. By the end of the exercise, he claims to already be generating solutions to multiple problems he had been trying to solve.

Kotler's second, more Rogan-appropriate, tactic is to go for a walk, drink a cup of coffee, and smoke a joint. Both methodologies have the ability to induce a nice cocktail of brain juices that facilitate flow, he claims. Flow and creativity are associated with the brain chemicals norepinephrine and dopamine. Together, the chemicals increase the signal-to-noise ratio in the brain, effectively helping pattern recognition, one of two components to creativity. Creativity, according to Kotler, is the combination of information acquisition (learning) and pattern recognition (making mental connections). Increasing flow, then, is like putting creativity on steroids.

Still, there are often other factors of entering flow, one of which is environment.

Tuning out the world is a key ingredient. Many writers, including both Kotler and Rogan as well as Michael Lewis (*The Blind Side*, *The Big Short*) and Ryan Holiday (*Ego Is the Enemy*, *The Obstacle Is the Way*) listen to one song or a single playlist on repeat for the entirety of their writing project.

Holiday unabashedly admits to ruining music for himself as he now exclusively uses it as a tool for dropping into his flow state. When writing, he picks a single song and plays it on repeat, often 300-400 times before exhausting it. To Holiday, the consistent background noise helps him focus.

"In my experience, it's not about quiet. It's about finding your zone," he said.[143]

Empirically, the odd habit checks out. The phenomenon of stochastic resonance holds that adding in more noise can actually clarify a signal. For example, the presence of (literal) background noise actually helps listeners identify a weak S.O.S. signal. This may be why many college students prefer to study in the library instead of their dorm rooms, where the slight buzz of activity actually helps them focus. A bit of chatter and noise may serve to clarify our thinking and help us find flow.

I tried Holiday's technique. To my embarrassment, I now have a (private) Spotify playlist of songs that I have listened to individually on repeat for hours on end while I write. My selection ranges from Vivaldi to Cardi B and, for better or for worse, it helped produce the words you are reading right now. For dense, technical material, I recommend songs without words, but if you play the same song over and over, or if you listen to Cardi B, English tends to lose its meaning anyway.

Adding repetitive music is one flow-triggering tactic, but the best methodologies will vary from person to person. Researchers at Kotler's Flow Research Collective organization have identified seventeen different triggering states, including novelty, complexity, having clear goals, pattern recognition, and risk, each of which introduce some amount of the right brain chemicals for flow.[144] Kotler recommends keeping a journal of times you've entered flow to help identify personal patterns in your psyche.

---

143. Ryan Holiday, "The Guilty, Crazy Secret That Helps Me Write," *Ryan Holiday* (blog), Ryan Holiday, updated April 14, 2014.

144. Troy Erstling, "What Are Flow Triggers? And How Do They Work?" *The Flow Research Collective*, Flow Research Collective, updated July 29, 2020.

Deep Work

Take the time to figure out your personal triggers. When it comes to exponential success, entering flow isn't a nice-to-have; it's a must-have. Georgetown University professor Cal Newport believes that deep work, his own term for the focused state required to enter flow, is essential for above-the-norm professional success.

"If you're not comfortable going deep for extended periods of time, it'll be difficult to get your performance to the peak levels of quality and quantity increasingly necessary to thrive professionally," he writes. "Unless your talent and skills absolutely dwarf those of your competition, the deep workers among them will outproduce you."[145]

Newport's particular mode of attack for doing deep work takes a via negativa, or "adding by subtracting," approach. Instead of asking what one can add to their life to enter flow, Newport wants to know what one can remove.

To start, he advocates the abolishment of all distractions. Deep workers are encouraged to delete social media, turn off notifications, and check email at the absolute minimum frequency. Specific time should be set aside for deep work, where interactions with others are unlikely to pull one out of their focus, Newport says.

One good thing about this process is that setting aside intentional work time won't eat up your whole day. Experienced deep workers tend to reach a maximum of four deep work hours per day and are likely to experience diminished returns after that.[146] For those of us with families, busy offices,

---

145. Cal Newport, *Deep Work*, (New York: Grand Central Publishing, 2016), 44.
146. Ibid.

and an active social life, though, four hours a day of solitary, focused work might sound like a lot. And anyway, isn't collaboration a key ingredient in producing exponential success? True, interfacing with lots of people in diverse environments is a surefire way to expose yourself to exciting ideas. Also, working with teams, having mastermind groups, and sourcing mentors and exemplars are all excellent tactics for success, up to a certain point. We'll talk about all of these in later chapters. But to truly enter flow, or deep work, working alone may be the ticket.

Notoriously introverted Apple co-founder Steve "Woz" Wozniak is an avid advocate of working alone.[147] When he worked at Hewlett-Packard, he'd arrive early in the morning and work alone in his cubicle. After eating dinner at home in the evenings, he'd drive back to the office and burn the midnight oil, working in the silence of the dark office to develop what would become the modern-day computer. He was alone when he successfully typed the first letters onto a keyboard that appeared on a screen, a monumental milestone in tech history on par with the invention of the Gutenberg printing press.[148]

Certainly, some personality types are more disposed to solo creation time than others. Wozniak was known for being shy, although early in his career he did take the time to attend hobbyist groups like the Homebrew Computer Club, where nerdy computer enthusiasts discussed various computer parts, and has since even appeared as a contestant on *Dancing With The Stars*.[149] Still, Woz is an avid supporter

---

147. Cain, *Quiet*, 73.
148. Ibid.
149. "Steve Wozniak." Dancing with the Stars Wiki. Fandom TV. Accessed February 13, 2021.

of solo creation time. "Artists work best alone," he says. He implores engineers and artists in particular to do their work by themselves. "Work alone. You're going to be best able to design revolutionary products and features if you're working on your own. Not on a committee. Not on a team."[150]

Having some level of introversion myself, I have always been drawn to stories of solo creation. As a teen, I was enraptured by the story of acoustic folk musician Justin Vernon writing his album *For Emma, Forever Ago*. In 2006, Vernon, who is widely known by the pseudonym Bon Iver, allegedly broke up with both his band and girlfriend in North Carolina to go hibernate alone in a remote Wisconsin cabin for a winter. Nursing himself through both mononucleosis and a liver infection in the cabin, Vernon hunted deer for food and spent his days toying around with soft folk melodies.[151]

Like a modern day Thoreau, Vernon emerged after several months of deep solo work with nine songs that became his first album under the Bon Iver name. Melodic, ethereal, and beautiful, the album went on to achieve platinum status and captured my teenage heart along with the world's.

The interesting thing about Vernon's prolific experience is that he not only removed the noise from his old social group and surroundings, but he added in completely new inputs. Just weeks before his exodus, he'd been working in a North Carolina sandwich shop and siphoning his money away in online poker games. He now credits the creation of his bestselling album to his change of scenery and lengthy introspective time at the cabin.

---

150. Cain, *Quiet*, 73.
151. Laura Barton, "Cabin Fever," *The Guardian*, Guardian News & Media Limited, May 14, 2008.

Both signal and noise are important here. For anyone who deals in creative or problem-solving work, diverse inputs can be a crucial component to success. Stepping back from the noise in order to enter flow state and hear the signal can be the final step in creating a tour de force. For Vernon, the Wisconsin winter was a fresh canvas for creativity. "When it's winter out there, there are no leaves on the trees and the pines are really tall, and there are lanes of light inside them, and bare hills, and so much space," he told *The Guardian*. "That space really did hand me a lot of ideas—ideas that I already had, but that I needed help with strengthening."[152]

Sometimes stepping away is what's needed for flow state. While a little bit of background noise, like the stochastic resonance of a buzzing coffee shop can be helpful, solitude is often the final factor to fall into place when doing deep and intense creative work. With the opportunity to maximize your output up to several hundred times, flow is a critical component to achieving exponential success. Learning how to drop into it, creating the space, and ultimately secluding yourself for hours of uninterrupted work will have compounding returns on effort in the long run. Taking the time to learn your flow triggers, whether it's long walks, joints, lonely cabins, or F-bombs, is an exercise well worth the effort.

---

152. Ibid.

CHAPTER 8

THE WHISPERS OF CITIES

Some environments squelch new ideas while some
environments seem to breed them effortlessly.

—STEVEN JOHNSON

Environment

I have a fantastic productivity technique for you. Clean your
desk. You'll be able to focus on your work better. And when
you've finished with your desk, clean your office. Now that
you mention it, the kitchen looks a little grungy, and there's
no possible way you'll be able to concentrate on your work
if you're thinking about the gross coffee mugs sitting in the
sink. It must be done.

I have spent weeks doing this: indulging the procrastina-
tion monster by pretending I'm creating a better environment
for myself.

The funny thing is: when properly cultivated, your environment actually is an incredible force-multiplier for success.

But it's easy to think you're changing something important when, in reality, it's inconsequential.

A typical self-help book would probably tell you to clean your desk, hang up motivational posters, and light a candle to *get in the zone*. But these tiny tweaks don't produce compounding results; in fact, they may fool you into thinking you're being more productive when, actually, they're mere distractions.

No candles, striking power poses, or binaural beats here: In this chapter, we'll explore the much larger factors that create Archimedes levers for success in your environment.

Hidden Messages

As much as creators and thinkers like to believe they could conduct their business in a vacuum, humans as social creatures are heavily influenced by their immediate environment. Placing yourself in an ideal physical location not only gives you the benefits of a place but ensures you are surrounded by people who will multiply your success. Just as your immediate circle influences your behaviors and lifestyle, the greater energy in a city amplifies this effect, for better or for worse.

In a funny way, hidden between the noise and traffic and sirens, cities tend to whisper. All day long, they tell people what to value and who to be. Y Combinator co-founder Paul Graham explains how location matters in his essay, "Cities and Ambition." According to Graham, a city like LA sends the message that people should be famous. Everyone cares about the size of your audience and if they've heard of you before. Cambridge, Massachusetts, by contrast, values intellect. "The people you find in Cambridge are not there by accident," Graham writes. "You have to make sacrifices to live there. It's expensive and somewhat grubby, and the weather's often bad. So the kind of people you find in Cambridge are the kind of people who want to live where the smartest people are, even if that means living in an expensive, grubby place with bad weather." Whereas Berkeley folks are just as smart, they care more about living well than intellectual prowess, Graham says.[153]

Now, these whispers should come as no surprise, because *of course* cities have different energies—that's why it's so fun to travel to different ones. The key thing to look out for is that the messages cities send may be different than you expect. San Franciscans want to know how powerful you are but in a far nerdier sense than LA. New York cares how much money and glamour you have in a far more classic sense than either San Francisco or Los Angeles. Bozeman, Montana locals want to know how many IPAs you can drink and still ski straight.

However small, these subtle messages can significantly affect the chances of achieving our chosen moonshots. Particularly in this age of remote work, we'd all like to think that we can perform at our highest level from anywhere, but this belief may be rooted more in desire than actual outcomes. Graham writes:

> How much does it matter what message a city sends? Empirically, the answer seems to be: a lot. You might think that if you had enough strength of mind to do great things, you'd be able to transcend your

---

153. Paul Graham, "Cities and Ambition," *Paul Graham* (blog), updated May 2008.

environment. Where you live should make at most a couple percent difference. But if you look at the historical evidence, it seems to matter more than that. Most people who did great things were clumped together in a few places…[154]

Far from the impenetrable, consistent entities we'd like to think we are, we are heavily influenced by the things our cities care about. We regress to the mean values of our environments. To some extent, we all know this intuitively. It's part of the reason we find story tropes like country-girl-becomes-international-pop-star (Hannah Montana, Taylor Swift) so compelling. We like to think we can break out of the molds our locations create for us.

In reality, if our ambitions don't line up with our homes, our chances of success dwindle. As tech policy reporter Tim Lee told *The Atlantic:*

> When I lived in DC and I told people I worked at a think tank, virtually everyone knew what that was and many were interested to know which one and what I did there. When I go to a party in St. Louis, the people I meet not only don't know what a think tank is, but a lot of them don't know what public policy is. I've taken to just telling people I'm a writer, which is something most people have heard of.[155]

Lee was lucky to be an adult and already settled into his career; kids with unconventional dreams have an even

---

154. Ibid.
155. Megan McArdle, "The Message of Cities," *The Atlantic*, Atlantic Media Company, July 18, 2008.

tougher time pursuing them when their communities don't understand and can't help them with the resources to try and accomplish them. Still, swimming against the current of what your location values at any age can take a psychological toll. You can almost hear the deep sigh that followed Lee's career explanations at parties.

We thrive where we're understood, but we also thrive when we have a great diversity of thoughts and ideas, which is why cities are often hubs for innovation.

What is it about cities that shapes our situations so much?

Idea Melting Pot

For those in professions where artistic creativity or creative problem-solving is required, moving to a metropolitan area can have compounding effects on your creative output ability.

City size has mathematically been shown to correlate with creativity. A team of scientists at the Santa Fe Institute decided to study creativity in relation to population size of cities and returned with fascinating results: the bigger the city, the more creative the people are. Even more striking is the fact that the correlation is stronger than linear; it compounds.[156]

The research team, led by theoretical physicist Geoffrey West, collected data points in cities associated with creativity and innovation. Data points included factors like R&D budgets, numbers of patents, creative professions, and inventors. When they compared the ratio of creative data points to city size they came to a surprising conclusion: Creativity scores rise disproportionately to the size of the city.

---

156. Johnson, *Where Good Ideas Come From,* 10.

"A city that was ten times larger than its neighbor wasn't ten times more innovative; it was *seventeen* times more innovative. A metropolis fifty times bigger than a town was 130 times more innovative," author Steven Johnson writes.[157] As it turns out, there are many factors about cities that have compounding effects. Just as with creativity, productivity was also shown to increase with city size in a nonlinear fashion. This is good news for anyone who's looking for a leg up in chasing success.

While we can't all pack up immediately and move to the nearest metropolitan innovation hub, the research indicates a positive change in environment can have compounding effects on success. The key question is: What is it about population density that increases outcomes like innovation and productivity? Are there ways to replicate these effects without moving somewhere new? The answer seems to be in the ways people interact with one another.

For example, the same increases in creativity aren't found in cities and neighborhoods with poor transportation infrastructure. Mobility is important. Unsurprisingly, this puts underprivileged communities at an even larger disadvantage. Spatial isolation practices like redlining keep these people from interacting with other groups, denying them the intellectual benefits of living in a diverse metropolitan area. The more difficult it is to traverse a given city, the more people are stuck in their own local networks without frequent opportunities to intermix with others and share ideas with one another. Poor transportation is perhaps why densely-packed but mobile San Francisco is recognized more for innovation than its sprawling, gridlocked sister city, Los Angeles. People

---

157. Ibid.

who live in their own bubbles, metropolitan or not, don't benefit from city life in the same way. While being idea-adjacent is good, active participation is even better. Research by the MIT Media Laboratory's Human Dynamics Lab indicates that face-to-face interaction increases productivity.[158, 159] The greater the "social-tie density," the average number of people that each resident of a city interacted with, the more productive the city was.

Regardless of where you live, at least two socio-environmental factors are at play that can dramatically increase both creativity and output: frequency of contact and diversity of interaction types with others. Even if you live in a small town in the country, these factors can be cultivated with proper attention.

To play off of Peter Drucker's famed "what gets measured gets managed" aphorism, what is understood can be curated. No matter where you live, spending depth of time with people you know and trust and spending breadth of time meeting new people is a good way to get the ol' creativity juices flowing.

Blogger and writing coach David Perell does the bulk of his writing preparation through having conversations with others. Before the pandemic, Perell attended discussion groups with people from different social circles three times a week. He prefers to spend his time having deep, meaningful conversations. "I basically only hang out with people for at least three hours," he told me. "It takes that time to get to the level of depth where you really begin to break new ground."

158. Wei Pan, et. al, "Urban Characteristics Attributable to Density-Driven Tie Formation," *Nature Communications* 4, no. 1 (2013).
159. Larry Hardesty. "Why Innovation Thrives in Cities." *MIT News*. Massachusetts Institute of Technology, updated June 4, 2013.

Perell is known for his longform essays that explore everything from business to religion to education. Oftentimes, he will record conversations with others and use the transcriptions as the foundations for writing pieces. Conversing expedites and uncovers ideas, he believes. "Speaking is thinking. When we share our ideas, we discover unexpected insights and unlock the hidden realms of suppressed thought and forgotten ideas. Through the unexpected randomness of conversation, we maximize intellectual serendipity and explore the contours of our own minds."[160]

While in-person conversations with a variety of different people may be the most powerful tool for creating mental synergy, the exchange of ideas is also available to anyone with internet access. We can now tap into the global hive mind and see millions of ideas from people around the globe. By watching lectures online, reading articles, attending virtual conferences, listening to podcasts, and participating on forums, idea sharing is no longer exclusive to people in highly mobile, diverse areas.

This framework calls into question breadth versus depth in relationships. Anecdotally, depth seems to bring the most meaning and long-term happiness to the table; however, the breadth of your connectivity does dictate the amount of opportunities that you come across. While people hear about the same opportunities as their close friends, second-level acquaintances are more often the reason we get new jobs. Large networks can be incredibly valuable. One study showed that every additional email contact an IBM employee had was

---

160. David Perell, "The Fruits of Friendship," *David Perell* (blog), January 19, 2021.

worth an added \$948 in revenue to the company.[161]

Empirically, well-connected people may get better opportunities, while people with deeper connections may find greater satisfaction in their relationships. A great way to bridge this gap is to aim to be "T" shaped, or to have few very deep friendships and to keep a broad, but more surface-level, social net on top.

Smart Adjacent

Carefully selecting the people you go deep with is paramount. American Entrepreneur Jim Rohn famously said that we are the average of the five people we surround ourselves with.[162] Our closest connections reveal our values and lifestyles and have the ability to reinforce or change the way we behave.

The principle is simple: If our closest friends play video games for thirteen hours a day and think kale and okra are *Star Trek* character names, not vegetables, it's unlikely that we'll be health and fitness fanatics. Adjacent lifestyles tend to match up over time, just like metronomes placed together will eventually sync to the same beat.[163] If we only hang out with Olympic athletes, chances are that physical health and

161. Eric Barker, *Barking up the Wrong Tree: The Surprising Science Behind Why Everything You Know About Success Is (Mostly) Wrong*, (New York: HarperOne, an imprint of HarperCollins Publishers, 2019) 128.

162. Melia Robinson, "Tim Ferriss: 'You Are the Average of the Five People You Most Associate with,'" *Business Insider*, Business Insider, last modified January 11, 2017.

163. "Synchronization of Metronomes," Harvard Natural Sciences Lecture Demonstrations, The President and Fellows of Harvard College, accessed February 17, 2021.

extreme self-discipline will (knowingly or not) become core components of our value system. Of course, you exhibit the same influence on your friends as they do on you, and you're more likely to pick friends who already share your values. It holds true, however, that humans have a tendency to regress to the mean, or adjust away from being an outlier, in their surroundings.[164]

The quality of the people around you determines the quality of your environment.

Having an intentionally curated peer group is perhaps one of the most critical components of success. As social creatures, we're trained to assimilate to the values of the people we care about. Choosing friends and partners who push us to be our best is imperative.

One particularly effective technique for curating an environment of inspiration and feedback is participating in a mastermind group. The term *mastermind* was reportedly coined by author Napoleon Hill in 1925, who spent years studying the likes of successful people like Thomas Edison, Theodore Roosevelt, and Henry Ford.[165] In business circles, a mastermind group is a small group of people, typically from different disciplines or who work at different companies, that congregate regularly to give professional support and tackle problems together. The idea is to form a peer-to-peer mentorship group of smart individuals with diverse perspectives.

One entrepreneur I spoke with has been attending his monthly mastermind group for four years. He describes it as the single most important technique for professional

164. "Regression Toward the Mean: An Introduction with Examples," *Farnam Street* (blog), Farnam Street Media Inc., accessed January 18, 2021.

165. Stephanie Burns, "7 Reasons To Join A Mastermind Group," *Forbes*, Forbes Magazine, updated October 21, 2013.

improvement that he has utilized in his work, as measured both in job performance and satisfaction. His mastermind group is intimate, composed of just three or four other entrepreneurs who help challenge each other, provide resources, and give each other feedback about the work they are doing. Starting or joining a mastermind group is a particularly effective practice for career advancement. Sometimes these kinds of groups come together organically, as with the "PayPal Mafia," the first team at PayPal. Since the company sold to eBay for $1.5 billion in 2002, the original players have helped each other start other wildly successful companies. Peter Thiel, the "don" of the infamous group, went on to start Palantier and Founders Fund. Reid Hoffman co-founded LinkedIn. Steve Chen, Chad Hurley, and Jawed Karim all co-founded YouTube. Jeremy Stoppelman and Russel Simmons founded Yelp. Elon Musk started Tesla, SpaceX, Neuralink, OpenAI, and The Boring Company.[166]

The success of these companies is at least in part due to the influence of the smart and talented group and the strong friendships within. Jawed Karim reportedly showed the concept for YouTube to a PayPal friend at a backyard barbeque.[167] The friend passed the idea along to Roelof Botha, a former PayPal executive who was then a partner at venture capital behemoth Sequoia Capital. Sequoia soon invested in YouTube, which went on to hire even more former PayPal employees. "YouTube is like a PayPal reunion," PayPal co-founder Max Levchin said.[168]

166. Peter Thiel, *Zero to One: Notes on Startups, or How to Build the Future*, (London: Virgin Books, 2014), 119.
167. Miguel Helft, "It Pays to Have Pals in Silicon Valley," *The New York Times*, October 17, 2006.
168. Ibid.

The success of PayPal and subsequent companies was no accident. Thiel carefully selected the first employees at PayPal to create a very specific environment of people who were passionate about the project and who were synergistic with the rest of the group. "We didn't assemble a mafia by sorting through resumes and simply hiring the most talented people. I had seen the mixed results of that firsthand... We set out to hire people who would actually enjoy working together. They had to be talented, but even more than that, they had to be excited about working specifically with us."[169]

Having friends in high places is useful, but surrounding yourself with ambitious, smart people has a proven exponential effect on personal success. Joining hobbyist groups, hosting masterminds, and seeking out driven individuals is a good place to start.

The Coral Reef of Humanity

The optimal place to position yourself is in the human equivalent of a coral reef, writes Johnson.[170] In otherwise nutrient-poor ocean areas, healthy reefs teem with diverse life forms interfacing with one another and forming symbiotic relationships. The diversity of life in coral reefs is so prolific that one quarter of all marine species live in them.

Cities—and the internet—are a lot like coral reefs. Ideas cross-pollinate across these mediums in the same way that nutrients and symbiotic relationships benefit from their own network effects. Thanks to the internet and libraries and the

---

169. Thiel, *Zero to One*, 119-120.
170. Johnson, *Where Good Ideas Come From*, 18.

general connectivity of our world, you don't have to live in a city to encounter a great diversity of ideas. Finding a place somewhere in the multifarious online or offline worlds of innovation is a great way to enhance creativity, output, and innovation. Bringing these ideas back to your close circle of confidants allows you to parse and synthesize the new information, get feedback, and add it to your world view.

By all means, close your office door and hunker down when you do your most creative work. This will help you break into flow state. But coming up for air once in a while is a great way to replenish the creative coffer. In many cases, inspiration and innovation come from interactions with others and from new experiences or learnings, so use your environment to your advantage. At the very least, do a little eavesdropping next time you're out on the town. You may learn a little more about what your city is whispering.

CHAPTER 9

GIVE & TAKE

———

For friendship is nothing else than an accord in all things, human and divine, conjoined with mutual goodwill and affection, and I am inclined to think that, with the exception of wisdom, no better thing has been given to man by the immortal gods.

—CICERO

"Networking" advice seems to be written in either a la-la-la happy-go-lucky sort of way ("let's all just help each other"), or with an icy-cold ruthlessness bordering on sociopathy.

—SEBASTIAN MARSHALL & KAI ZAU

Having dropped out of college a semester shy of graduating, James found himself doing standup comedy for $7.50 a show in LA. He'd dreamed of performing on the hit show *Saturday Night Live* since he was a kid, back in the days when his parents taped the show and let him watch *the clean parts*. In college, James had frequently skipped out on parties to watch it, never wanting to miss a minute.[171]

After cutting his teeth in the standup scene for a while, James finally got the call; he was invited to an audition with SNL. Live in New York's famed comedy club, Comic Strip Live, James performed a bit about Troll Dolls—and totally bombed. "It was terrible," he recounted later. "I couldn't get the crowd going, they didn't quite know what I was talking about, and I rushed into it. I was so nervous."[172]

Needless today, he didn't get hired. A year later, however, SNL reached back out. They wanted him to audition again, this time on the SNL set in front of the notoriously intimidating executive producer of the show, Lorne Michaels.[173] Despite words of caution from friends, James went out on a limb during his audition and did an Adam Sandler impression. To his delight, he looked down to see Michaels laughing.[174]

It was 1998 and James was hired as a performer on SNL. In his first weeks, producer Marci Klein gave James some of the best advice he would receive in his career: After every show, go and thank Michaels for the opportunity. "And I did," James said. "I thanked him after every single show. And by the third show, he probably got tired of me coming up. He was like, 'Sit down, come have a drink.'"[175] The post-show

171. Arie Levy, "Not Jerry Seinfeld," *New York Magazine,* New York Magazine, October 18, 1999.

172. Mandi Kerr, "Jimmy Fallon's Impression of Adam Sandler Got Him Cast on 'Saturday Night Live,'" Showbiz Cheat Sheet, updated May 26, 2020.

173. Richard Feloni, "How Jimmy Fallon Made It to 'The Tonight Show' Through Exceptional Networking," *Business Insider,* Business Insider, updated November 6, 2014.

174. Levy, "Not Jerry Seinfeld," 1999.

175. Andrew Goldman, "Jimmy Fallon's 7 Rules for Success," *Men's Journal,* A360 Media, accessed January 25, 2021.

chats soon turned into a genuine friendship, one that few actors had been able to achieve with the legendary producer. James went on to spend six years at SNL before pursuing other opportunities, growing and nurturing his friendship with Michaels all the while. In 2013, Michaels had a seat to fill on a well-known late night talk show for which he had been newly hired as an executive producer. It's no surprise that he offered the job to his longtime friend, James.[176]

The power of networking worked its magic, and our hero, James, "Jimmy" Fallon would go on to take the reins of the world's longest-running talk show, *The Tonight Show*.

Networking

Handshake-riddled cocktail parties, sterile "introduction" emails, and a pervasively privileged you-scratch-my-back-I'll-scratch-yours culture of using people to get ahead has given networking a bad name. Those who fall behind are left behind, and the idea of helping one another out has become a perverse game of breathless name-dropping and who's-who.

Still, it would be myopic to ignore the enormous role social connections play in both business and personal success. Authentic interpersonal relationships are perhaps one of the biggest factors of exponential achievement, but the key word is authentic; nobody likes the person who obsessively collects names of business contacts like they're going out of style.

Sincerity and true desire for connection are imperative to cultivating a high-functioning personal network. This chapter won't be a how-to about networking; there are innumerable

---

176. Feloni, "How Jimmy Fallon," 2014.

books and resources already on the topic. If you need instructions on how to give a firm-but-not-too-firm handshake, you've come to the wrong place (my palms are often damp and cold). Instead, we'll explore some key concepts to expand your mental model of networking. We'll examine how 25 percent of people bring success to everyone in their vicinity and how computers learn to trust one another, as well as dispelling a few myths, like the absolute necessity of mentorship.

Give & Take

We know that surrounding yourself with *good* and *helpful* people is a great way to boost success, but what exactly do these kinds of people look like, and how do you find folks who will actually give you a helping hand?

Adam Grant, an organizational psychologist and tenured professor at the University of Pennsylvania studied over thirty thousand people in workplaces and colleges around the globe to understand how different personality types affect culture and productivity. During the course of his extensive research, Grant identified three different categories of people in collaborative environments: givers, takers, and matchers.[177]

Givers made up about a quarter of the population, Grant discovered. Incredibly generous and helpful by nature, givers are people who are willing to spend ample amounts of their own time and resources helping others without the expectation of reciprocation. They are altruistic to a fault. Most of us are lucky to have a few givers in our lives.

---

177. Adam Grant, "Are You a Giver or a Taker?" TED, TED Conferences, updated November 2016.

Takers, by contrast, accept help from others but rarely offer it in return. Though not necessarily mean-spirited, these folks are intensely focused on their own work and aren't as group-oriented. "Not all takers are narcissists," Grant said in his TED talk. "Some are just givers who got burned one too many times. Then there's another kind of taker that we won't be addressing today, and that's called a psychopath." Grant found 19 percent of the people he studied fell into the taker category.[178]

The final, and largest, category was the matchers. Matchers believe in equal reciprocation between parties. This group, comprising 56 percent of the total, is willing to give as long as they feel their favors will be returned. They'll happily help you out, as long as you write them an I.O.U. These justice warriors, to no surprise, absolutely despise takers. The only group who hates takers more than matchers are other takers.

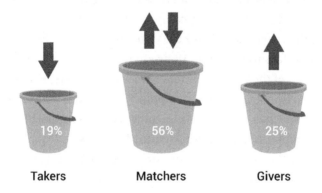

Takers   Matchers   Givers

Understanding these categories is useful for several reasons. First, it becomes apparent that you should fill your life or your business with as many givers as possible. "The more

---

178. Ibid.

often people are helping and sharing their knowledge and providing mentoring, the better organizations do on every metric we can measure," Grant said.[179] Givers, in other words, are Archimedes levers for *everything*. In businesses, Grant found that a high proportion of givers was correlated with increased profits, customer satisfaction, and employee retention. They added to the company's strengths and made the organizations even stronger. Just as rising tides lift all boats, givers increase the achievement of everyone around them.

Generous and giving as they are, givers run the risk of serious burnout. They rely heavily on the support around them, and as a result, will either thrive or nosedive in group environments. When it comes to success, givers occupy both the high and low tails of the bell curve. When Grant studied engineers, he found that givers were both the most and least productive people at their engineering jobs. The same pattern occurred in medical students. Med student givers had both the worst and best test scores, compared to matchers and takers.

What seemed to make the difference between high and low-performing givers? Their environment. If givers are drained of their energy by takers, everyone suffers. However, givers rise above the pack and propel everyone in the vicinity forward when their environment is set up to support them. Well-supported givers are Archimedes levers.

As either a boss, colleague, or friend, supporting the givers in your circles by giving them resources, checking in to prevent burnout, and giving them permission to work on their own work (without assisting others) is important to ensure their success as well as your own.[180]

---

179. Ibid.
180. Ibid.

Step one: Love thy givers. Step two: If you see a taker, run. When it comes to networks and relationships, everyone has their merits. However, takers have been shown to be exponentially *bad* for achievement. Takers are known for rising very quickly in their careers—and falling just as fast. Even worse, they bring others down with them. Instead of rising tides, takers are like tsunami waves that lift boats up before smashing them down onto rocks. In his research, Grant found that the impact of a taker had 200-300 percent higher negative impact on company culture than the positive impact of a giver, meaning you would need two to three givers to counterbalance the bad of one taker. It's worth going to great lengths to avoid spending time with takers, and by all means, don't hire one if you can avoid it.

The most significant force multiplier for success, however, is to become more of a giver yourself. Help people around you selflessly and often. Certainly, spend the necessary and adequate time on your own personal goals, but even spending a few minutes each day lifting up others around you is the most effective way to build strong, lasting connections and raise the caliber of achievement in your groups and networks. Ultimately, the best networks are built on friendships and mutual reciprocity.

Mentors vs. Exemplars

Surrounding yourself with thoughtful, high-caliber friends is a guaranteed win. But what about seeking out a mentor to ramp up your game even further?

There's much ado about mentors these days. Finding a mentor is like the new Pokémon GO: Everyone is in a mad dash to catch 'em all. Large corporations and universities alike have mentor-matching programs, and there are even specialized apps and platforms to help people find them on-demand. Mentors work really well if you know what you want to do or if you are already on a traditional career path. If you go into a field like real estate or law, having a senior agent or partner take you under their wing, show you the ropes, and introduce you around is invaluable. In some fields and companies, mentorship is the easiest way to rise through the ranks and learn quickly. Compared to non-mentored employees, mentees report greater career outcomes, including more promotions and greater job satisfaction.[181]

The idea of mentorship, however, is often exclusive to those without connections, and finding a good mentor can be exceedingly difficult. Not everyone has the built-in social ties to get the best mentor, the confidence to ask them for help, or even the industry chosen in which to search for one. Some experienced individuals actively avoid mentorship relationships. Though he extolls the benefits of them and even wrote a book about mentors, writer and podcaster Tim Ferriss once called mentors "unpaid consultants for life."[182]

Until you do or don't find a mentor to help expedite success, a more actionable strategy is to cultivate a tribe of *exemplars.*

Exemplars are the people in your friend group, family, or close circle who you admire and intentionally choose to connect with out of admiration. They're the up-close role models in our lives. Knowingly or not, their traits, habits,

---

181. Lauren Bidwell, "Why Mentors Matter: A Summary of 30 Years of Research," *SAP*, SAP, accessed January 26, 2021.

182. Tim Ferriss, "The Tim Ferriss Show Transcripts: Esther Perel (#241)," *The Tim Ferriss Show* (blog), Tim Ferriss, updated June 1, 2018.

and behaviors can and will rub off organically and silently, allowing you to grow and achieve far more than you could have on your own. Part of this is human nature, and part is due to a handy statistical concept called regression to the mean, which we touched on in the last chapter. The more you hang out with smart, kind, driven, and successful people, the more likely you are to embody those traits, lest you start to become a statistical outlier. It's unlikely that you'll hang out at the lower tail of the bell curve forever if your peers are far ahead of you. Nature doesn't favor outliers for long.

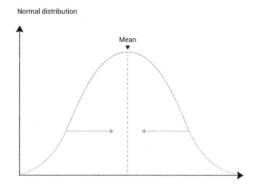

Normal distribution

Mean

The great thing about exemplars is that they're not hard to find. Ultraworking cofounders Sebastian Marshall and Kai Zau write about exemplars in their book, *Gateless*. Straying from the classic mentorship model, Marshall and Zau highlight the importance of finding people at any point in their journey who embody the values that you care about, regardless of age or professional title.[183]

---

183. Sebastian Marshall and Kai Zau, *Gateless*, Sebastian Marshall and Kai Zau (2014), 188.

Whereas mentorship often includes a power disparity (professional to amateur, older to younger), exemplars can be of any experience level or age. Exemplars display a trait or traits that you value and want to nurture in yourself. Optimism, critical thinking, courage, determination, loyalty, or great communication skills are common traits to seek out. The convenient thing about exemplars is that, unlike mentors, exemplars are all around us. "Networking is not about finding someone who can help you right this second. It's about establishing a relationship that can one day benefit both of you. And often the best people to do that with aren't the busy, important people. You want to meet the people who aren't well known but should be and will be. It's not about who has the biggest megaphone," author Ryan Holiday writes.[184] Exemplars are often the friends and colleagues in the same or adjacent social circles who can pass relevant opportunities your way and support you effectively because they're going through the same trials and tribulations that you are.

That's not to say that exemplarship is solely for young people. Bill Gates and Warren Buffett have a legendary friendship and both have expressed how much they've learned from one another. Each was already successful when they met (and neither of them particularly wanted to meet one another), but they hit it off right away, lending each other books and swapping investment advice. Neither one was a mentor to

---

184. Ryan Holiday, "23 Things I Learned About Writing, Strategy And Life From Tim Ferriss," Medium, Mission.org, updated October 19, 2018.

the other, but each was an exemplar, giving the other man a model of how to gracefully handle fame, wealth, and genius.[185] Research tells us that informal mentorship, like the kind you get from close friends and exemplars, is actually far more effective than structured, businesslike mentorship. This may be why formal mentoring programs don't produce the same kinds of results as organic mentoring relationships. Unlike motor oil, new and synthetic isn't actually better. The longer the trust builds, the more both parties get in return. Like AngelList cofounder Naval Ravikant said:

Relationships offer a good example of compound interest. Once you've been in a good relationship with somebody for a while—whether it's business or romantic—life gets a lot easier because you know that person's got your back. You don't have to keep questioning. If I'm doing a deal with someone I've worked with for twenty years and there is mutual trust, we don't have to read the legal contracts. Maybe we don't even need to create legal contracts; maybe we can do it with a handshake. That kind of trust makes it very easy to do business.[186]

Filling your inner circle with exemplars of different traits allows you to saturate your mind with the best characteristics you see in others. Additionally, it ensures your primary interpersonal connections share your values.

---

185. Shana Lebowitz and Debanjali Bose, "Inside the Almost 30-Year Friendship of Bill Gates and Warren Buffett, Who Didn't Even Want to Meet and Now Have Each Other on Speed Dial," *Business Insider*, Business Insider, updated September 3, 2020.
186. Naval Ravikant, "Compounding Relationships Make Life Easier," *Naval* (blog), updated December 29, 2019.

Personal Board of Directors

One of the best relationship-building techniques I have learned came from an exemplar friend of mine. Over the years, he has aggregated a list of people he trusts and admires that he wants to keep updated about his personal and professional progress. Roughly once a month, he sends them an update email about what he is working on, how it is going, and things he could use help with. He calls these people his personal board of directors.

The emails don't necessitate a response, but they are an effective way of keeping important people up-to-date about his life. Occasionally, someone on the list is a perfect fit for helping him with a particular project or issue. Most of the time, the emails serve simply to keep him and his goals on other people's radar, in case compatible opportunities should come along. Occasionally, someone will signal boost his accomplishments or requests to their network. Personal board of directors emails follow a cardinal rule of networking: *always tell your network what you're doing and what you need help with.* Closed mouths don't get fed, and people can't provide the jet fuel for your moonshot if they don't know you've built a rocket.

The hardest part of creating a personal board, particularly for people like me who have Christopher McCandless-levels of individuality and prefer to accomplish things without any outside help, is getting over the fear of bothering people. It's not an uncommon fear.

"I think a lot of first-time makers (i.e., founders, writers, publishers, podcasters) shy away from sending update emails because they have a fear of rejection," writes Zak Slayback, a principle at 1517 Fund. "They fear people unsubscribing from lists or not liking what they are working on or getting angry that they are being emailed by this person. Or they assume that people would just reach out if they were interested. Neither of these are really true."[187] You're going to meet a lot of people who can't immediately help you but want to help you at some point down the line, Slayback told me. Many of them are busy people and won't remember to check in on you. It's your job to stay top-of-mind so they can help you when it becomes possible. Ultimately, the people in your network want to see you succeed.

When writing this book, I had an incredible community of early supporters who helped me choose my cover design and even edit chapters. Though asking for help sometimes felt like pulling teeth, this book would not be the same if I hadn't sent them update emails with progress reports and requests for help.

Unobtrusively keeping people updated about your life and goals is one of the easiest, best ways to cultivate a group of people around you who will support and help you. As an alternative to traditional mentorship, both exemplars and a personal board of directors are great ways to start effectively building your network—without being annoying.

Radical Ownership

Humans are a highly conflict-prone species. Ever notice how couples fight on vacations? Or how children are well-behaved until they melt down at their own birthday parties? When

---

187. Zak Slayback, "How to Write Update Emails That Help, Not Annoy," *Zak Slayback* (blog), accessed January 25, 2021.

everything is going right, we have a tendency to poke the bear and make it go wrong.

My grandmother used to call this an "imp light." As a child, whenever I'd get a mischievous look on my face, she could tell. "Your imp light is on," she'd say to me, smiling. I always wondered if she could see a little lightbulb hovering above my head that would turn on when I was about to get into trouble. I looked hard for that lightbulb, never knowing how my intentions had been so transparent. I've never been good at hiding my feelings, but in some ways, it has been more of an asset than a liability. In relationships, conflict is inevitable, but transparency and vulnerability are important parts of your toolkit when times get rough. Combining these characteristics with responsibility and ownership is a royal flush.

An incredibly high-leverage trait is radical ownership—taking complete responsibility for everything in your life, even factors that may seem out of your control. If someone cuts you off in traffic, you can take ownership of your reaction to it. Will you let it ruin your day? Will you later pick a fight with your spouse because you want to offload your indignant and enraged emotions? Radical ownership means taking full responsibility. Perhaps, when the car cut you off, you were speeding. You could have given the car ahead of you more space. Perhaps you hadn't been paying full attention to the road.

Taking ownership avoids the blame game. While blaming others can feel satisfying and protects our own egos, it does little to foster trust and goodwill in relationships. This kind of behavior destroys friendships, and even more so, teams. Teams must feel that their leader has got their back and will hold themselves to an even higher standard of responsibility than everyone else. This is a nod to the "no bad teams, only bad leaders" mindset used by Navy SEALS to designate accountability.

Retired Navy SEAL Jocko Willink talks about this principle in his book, *Extreme Ownership*. One night, deep in the fog of war in one of the most dangerous neighborhoods of Ramadi, Iraq, Willink's Navy SEAL team suffered a fatal miscommunication. Through a number of combined errors, the troop that Willink led committed an act of blue-on-blue, their code term for friendly fire. Bullets were fired from groups both inside and outside of a building, each assuming they were combatting enemy insurgents, when really they were comrades.[188]

In the end, one man died and several were wounded. Fratricide is considered one of the most heinous and avoidable acts of war—a scenario all military troops are trained to avoid. In particular, Willink wrote, it's an event that incredibly-specialized SEAL teams should be able to prevent at all costs.

For Willink, the event was personally and professionally devastating. Following the mission, all operations of Willink's team were shut down and senior commanding officers were flown in to investigate the tragedy. Willink was instructed to create a presentation for the senior officers to explain what went wrong. As he stood in front of his own SEAL unit and the higher-ups who were likely to discipline him and relieve him of his job, he realized something about the incident:

It wasn't the fault of the sniper team that fired at the assumed enemy.

---

188. Jocko Willink and Leif Babin. *Extreme Ownership: How U.S. Navy SEALs Lead and Win*. (New York: St. Martin's Press, 2017) 45-55.

It wasn't the fault of the radioman who delayed communicating the coordinates of the troops.

It wasn't the fault of the friendly Iraqi soldiers who traversed outside of their designated zone.

Willink took a deep breath. "There is only one person to blame for this," he said, "Me. I am the commander. I am responsible for the entire operation. As the senior man, I am responsible for every action that takes place on the battlefield. There is no one to blame but me."[189]

Though Willink wasn't actually at the scene of the blue-on-blue, he knew he could have prevented it. He could have made his teams double-check that their coordinates had been communicated accurately and he could have collaborated more closely with the Iraqi team. Though he might have passed the responsibility for the career-ending error onto any member of his squad, he chose to bear the burden alone, as a leader.

As it turned out, owning up to his mistakes instead of shirking them off indicated to the senior leadership that he was capable of continuing his job as SEAL commander. His SEAL team unit grew to trust him even more and became the most highly decorated Special Operations Unit of the Iraq War.

"Looking back, it is clear that, despite what happened, the full ownership I took of the situation actually increased the trust my commanding officer and master chief had in me. If I had tried to pass the blame on to others, I suspect I would have been fired—deservedly so. The SEALs in the troop, who did not expect me to take the blame, respected the fact that I had taken full responsibility for everything that had happened. They knew it was a dynamic situation caused by a

---

189. Ibid.

multitude of factors, but I owned them all," Willink said.[190]

Radical ownership, or as Willink calls it, extreme ownership, is one of the highest forms of integrity. It commands respect, which is hard to gain and easily lost. It demands integrity, altruism, and taking responsibility, which are all qualities of givers. Developing this skill is a highly effective Archimedes lever to elevate your current relationships as well as a method of making yourself an invaluable member of an organization, an amicable spouse, or a great friend.

Drop the Ego

The common thread between being a giver, attracting exemplars, and taking radical ownership is dropping the ego. Taking steps to reduce one's own selfish desires can have compounding effects on both relationships and success.

One benefit of suppressing individualistic desires is fostering a culture of collaboration and sharing. When people are open with their ideas and eager to help, creativity and innovation can flow more freely. Consider the invention of something almost everyone has within arm's reach at home: Post-it Notes. Today's version of these sticky little pieces of paper was created by Dr. Spencer Silver, a scientist at Minnesota-based Fortune 500 company, 3M. At the time, Silver was working on a project to create a strong adhesive. Unfortunately, he found himself in a rather (un)sticky situation: His adhesives weren't turning out strong at all. In fact, they came apart quite easily.[191]

---

190. Ibid.

191. "History Timeline: Post-it® Notes," Post-It Brand, 3M, accessed January 26, 2021.

3M has always placed a strong emphasis on innovation. Boasting over one hundred thousand patents and filing an incredible four-thousand-plus new ones each year, 3M encourages employees to try new things and share their results, even if they are considered failures.[192] Silver embraced this mindset wholeheartedly. Though his adhesive was an objective failure in the context of his project, he wasn't shy about sharing his findings with others in the company. Without letting his ego hold him back, Silver spent several years telling his colleagues about his failed experiment that had produced something mildly interesting. Eventually, Silver discussed his discovery in a lecture that happened to be attended by another 3M scientist named Art Fry.[193]

Silver had a solution but no problem to apply it to. Fry had a problem. During his weekly church choir practices, Fry had been experiencing a regular annoyance: on Wednesday, he'd mark the upcoming hymns he would be singing at the Sunday service with scraps of paper. By the time Sunday rolled around, his makeshift bookmarks would have all fallen out.

When Fry saw Silver's lecture, Fry had a eureka moment: He realized Silver's weak adhesive would be perfect as a temporary bookmark. Before long, Silver and Fry teamed up to create Post-it Notes. They shared their invention widely with colleagues, to great success. "I thought, what we have here isn't just a bookmark. It's a whole new way to communicate," Fry remembers.[194] He was right. After several iterations, Post-it notes were a massive hit in the market. Thanks to 3M's culture of sharing and Silver's willingness to drop

192. "3M's '100-Patent Woman' Audrey Sherman Explains How She Did It," 3M News Center, 3M Company, updated January 14, 2019.
193. "History Timeline," 2021.
194. Ibid.

his ego and share his failed experiment, 3M ended up with a breakout product.

Altruism vs. Self-Interest

Dropping your ego is good for humility and building rapport with others, but how do we make sure we stand up for ourselves when it's necessary? The answer may lie in a famous game theory paradox.

Scientists studying decision analysis use a game called the Prisoner's Dilemma to try and understand more about human trust.[195] The game goes like this: two people rob a bank. There are no witnesses, and when they are caught, they're immediately separated by police and placed in different interrogation rooms. The police give the perps some options:

1. If both prisoners remain silent and refuse to testify to incriminate the other, they are convicted of a lesser crime and each sentenced to one year in prison.
2. If both prisoners testify to incriminate the other, they are both sentenced to three years in prison for co-committing the crime.
3. If Prisoner #1 testifies to incriminate Prisoner #2 and Prisoner #2 remains silent, Prisoner #2 is sentenced to five years and Prisoner #1 walks free.

The prisoners aren't able to talk with one another before giving their statements and it's assumed that there isn't any

---

195. Charles Potters, ed. "Prisoner's Dilemma," *Investopedia*, Investopedia, accessed January 1, 2021.

loyalty between them. Their only chance at not serving any prison time is to incriminate the other person; however, if both pull the trigger against the other, they could spend three times as many years in prison than if they had both remained silent.

If you were a robber, what would you do? Do you stay silent and hope your accomplice does the same? Do you incriminate your partner and hope they take one for the team? How much do you trust your partner-in-crime?

The Prisoner's Dilemma was of particular interest to a man named Robert Axelrod in the early eighties. Axelrod was a professor of political science and public policy at the University of Michigan, and later a McArthur fellow.[196] He wanted to definitively find the strategy that would have the best outcome if the Prisoner's Dilemma was run multiple times, so he crafted up an experiment to test the problem. Axelrod created a computer program that would run hundreds of iterations of the game, testing different methodologies to see which strategies of incrimination or cooperation would lead a computer program to benefit the majority of the time. He invited researchers in game theory, psychology, math, economics, and sociology all across the world to devise and submit algorithms to battle it out.[197] The fourteen chosen algorithms were pitted against each other, against a program that would randomly cooperate and incriminate the other, and also against a clone of themselves.

---

196. Robert Axelrod, *The Evolution of Cooperation*, Stanford Engineering, (New York: Basic Books, 1984).

197. Eric Barker, *Barking up the Wrong Tree: The Surprising Science Behind Why Everything You Know About Success Is (Mostly) Wrong*, (New York: HarperOne 2019) 50.

The algorithms were all trained to behave differently in the Prisoner's Dilemma game and they had a whole range of different personalities. Some were selfish and ruthless; they'd throw their fellow criminal under the bus in all or most of the game iterations. Some were devious and would monitor the other program's behavior and look for weaknesses. Others were rather generous, giving the benefit of the doubt to the other program and rarely incriminating them at all.

Axelrod ran hundreds of iterations with the fourteen computer programs and discovered something shocking. The algorithm that won wasn't what anyone would expect. It was deceivingly simple, only two lines of code. The findings were so surprising that Axelrod went back to the scientific community and asked them to provide more algorithms. The researchers were able to review the results of the first tournament and build upon the existing algorithms or create completely new ones.

Axelrod sourced sixty-three more algorithms to try out.[198] Again, he ran hundreds of iterations with the programs and let them battle. Though it was competing against programs that were more complex and had been built on information from the previous trial, the same program emerged a winner: TFT. TFT was built on a simple concept: Tit for Tat. It would give the opposing program the benefit of the doubt in the first round and then *copy every single move* the other program made in the previous round. If Program X cooperated, TFT cooperated in the next round. If Program X was ruthless, TFT was ruthless right back.

198. *Stanford Encyclopedia of Philosophy*, s.v. "Prisoner's Dilemma," by Steven Kuhn, updated April 2, 2019.

What was it about the simple, two-line program that triumphed over every single algorithm submitted from scientists around the world? Axelrod analyzed Tit for Tat and found four outstanding principles that helped it emerge the winner of the Prisoner's Dilemma scenario.

1. TFT always started off by playing nice. It was never one to take the first swing, and likely built up some virtual robot goodwill.
2. It wasn't too nice. TFT wasn't going to be pushed around by bullies. It coldly provided swift justice when provoked.
3. TFT was reliable. It never threw curveballs and its behavior was clear and predictable.
4. It displayed unrelenting forgiveness. As soon as another program began acting cooperatively, TFT left all resentment in the past and reciprocated with kindness.

As soon as the other programs learned TFT wasn't going to take advantage of them but wouldn't be pushed around, they began searching for outcomes that were mutually beneficial. TFT rode this goodwill train all the way to the finish line.

What does this teach us about networks and relationships? Cooperation is king. Everyone needs a helping hand on their moonshot journey, and the best way to get one is to give one. Finding a comfortable place between being a giver and being a matcher places you in the same strategic goldilocks zone that Tit-for-Tat used to find success.

True success in networks and relationships comes to those who work for it and to those who try actively to be decent human beings and take ownership of their actions. The beautiful thing is that there is no experience required. We all have the freedom to choose how to interact and when to help and when to drop our egos. As David Foster Wallace said in his famous 2005 Kenyon College commencement speech, "The really important kind of freedom involves attention and awareness and discipline and being able truly to care about other people and to sacrifice for them over and over in myriad petty, unsexy ways every day."[199]

Networking, done right, is not sexy. It's not business cards and martinis and informational interviews. A great boss once told me, "I make everyone around me rich." I watched it happen. He was generous with his time and always made introductions between friends to land them in mutually beneficial working relationships. He was a strategic giver from the heart, and people loved him for it. A rising tide lifts all boats.

---

199. *Lynn Skittle,* "This Is Water—Full version—David Foster Wallace Commencement Speech," updated May 29, 2013, video, 22:43.

CHAPTER 10

THE BRAIN OUTSIDE
YOUR BRAIN

———

They belonged to a continuous effort to make sense
of things, for the world was full of signs: you could
read your way through it; and by keeping an account
of your readings, you made a book of your own, one
stamped with your personality.

—ROBERT DARNTON

A Web of Zettels

In his lifetime, German social theorist Niklas Luhmann
(1927-1998) wrote over seventy books. Inconceivably, he also
produced four hundred scholarly articles, including over

two hundred unpublished manuscripts, all with a typewriter.[200, 201] His incredible output was of such a high caliber that he is thought of as one of the most important sociologists of the century. But how was one man able to be so prolific? He created his own internet.

Luhmann's genius came by devising a coded system for knowledge, called a *zettelkasten*. The concept, meaning "note box" in German, is a collection of index cards that acts as a filing and categorizing system for information. The note-taking system was pioneered in the sixteenth century, but Luhmann took it to a whole new level.

Luhmann wrote quotes, facts, thoughts, and stories on the cards, carefully tagging each one with a serial number so it could be easily found. The cards were stored in boxes with cards of similar topics, thousands of which soon amassed as Luhmann researched, learned, and read about topics ranging from mass media to ecology to love.[202] Over the course of his career, he created some ninety thousand zettel notecards, each with their own idea or fact written on them. This wasn't just a fancy rolodex: The most crucial part of the process is that, beyond the boxed categories, there wasn't any organization at all.

How can this be?

Let's say you love the quote that topped Chapter 1, "The best way to predict the future is to invent it," by computer pioneer, Alan Kay. You want to store this line to use it another

---

200. David Seidl and Hannah Mormann, "Niklas Luhmann as Organization Theorist," *Oxford Handbook of Sociology, Social Theory and Organization Studies*, January 2015, 125-57.

201. "The Literary Estate of Niklas Luhmann," Faculty of Sociology, University of Bielefeld, accessed February 1, 2021.

202. Seidl and Mormann, ""Niklas Luhmann as Organization Theorist," 2015.

time, but you don't know when or where you'll need it again. What's the best way to categorize it? Do you file it under Quotes, Inventions, Computers, Alan Kay, or even a general theme, like Future or Inspirational? Kay worked at Apple, Disney, Atari, et. al. Would you file it under any of those? With the zettelkasten method, the quote can be saved and tagged with information from each one of those categories as a little code in the corner of the index card, so no matter if you find yourself writing about Disney or computer programming, you can always find it. This is the principle behind the zettelkasten, the pioneer methodology of networked thought: ideas don't have a hierarchy. Unlike bulleted lists, the notes can be arranged and rearranged without consequence. By arranging and combining different ideas, Luhmann used these cards as the basis of his varied and prolific works, the information from his past and present research always at his fingertips.

The reason networked thought is so effective is because, as much as humans love neat organization, we don't think in hierarchies. The neurons in our brains are organized in a tree-branch formation, spidering outward and connecting or disconnecting with different pathways depending on which ones are used most. Our thoughts occur in the same fashion: tangential and interconnected. Just as the blockchain concept decentralized money, the zettelkasten decentralized thought.

When information is arranged in a flat structure, you don't have to dig through bulky categories to get to the information you want.

Consider my kimchi fried rice recipe. If I'm at the grocery store and want to quickly recall what to buy, I simply locate the memory of making the dish in my mind. From that central memory, my thoughts will spider off in the directions of the ingredients added. Rice, kimchi, soy sauce... sauces... oh, right! Toasted sesame oil! Had my brain been organized hierarchically, finding the right ingredient might look something like this:

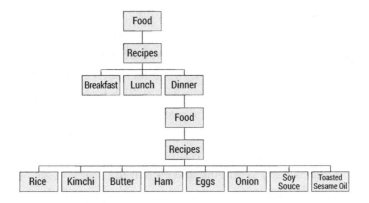

If the only way to access these ingredients in my mind was to pass through the doors of all the preceding categories, it would take forever to find any information at all. The most intuitive method of storing information is instead imitating the way our brains already work. As philosopher and psychologist William James wrote in 1880:

> Instead of thoughts of concrete things patiently following one another in a beaten track of habitual suggestion, we have the most abrupt cross-cuts and transitions from one idea to another... in a word, we seem suddenly introduced into a seething caldron of ideas, where everything is fizzling and bobbing about in a state of bewildering activity, where partnerships can be joined or loosened in an instant, treadmill

routine is unknown, and the unexpected seems the only law.[203]

The way the kimchi fried rice recipe is actually stored in my brain looks something like this:

The internet is arranged much in the same way as our brains. Pages link and backlink bi-directionally, allowing us to go down rabbit holes of learning and waste entire Sunday afternoons whenever we please. Unlike the internet, however, our neurons have a built-in *use it or lose it* heuristic. Neglected thoughts and memories have a nasty habit of disappearing into thin air.

Luhmann didn't store ninety thousand independent facts in his mind. They would have been lost as quickly as he learned them. He used a system of external networked thought, and through this, was able to exponentially increase his output. Like Charlie Munger said:

> You can't really know anything if you just remember isolated facts and try and bang 'em back. If the facts don't hang together on a latticework of theory, you don't have them in a usable form. You may have noticed students who just try to remember and pound back what is remembered. Well, they fail in school and in life. You've got to hang experience on a latticework of models in your head.[204]

---

203. William James, "Great Men, Great Thoughts, and the Environment," *Atlantic Monthly*, October 1880.
204. Andy Walker, "5 Mental Models For Investing & Everyday Life," *Augury*, Augury, April 18, 2020.

As we'll uncover, a technique called personal knowledge management is the latticework, the key to unlocking the next wave of incredible innovation. Am I suggesting that you start taking notes on ninety thousand pieces of paper? Not quite. In this chapter, we'll explore how you can use a zettelkasten-inspired system to compound your knowledge. First, however, let's examine how the brightest minds in history have tackled the challenge.

History's Best Kept Secret

Humans have been making records of things since the beginning of time. From cave paintings to hieroglyphics, we've always had an instinctive need to materialize what's in our brains. Without systematic organization, however, this knowledge often remains unconnected and siloed from making the serendipitous combinations that result in innovation and ultimately, exponential success.

Though record keeping has been around since humans could write—Plutarch's records of Archimedes' bath time adventures being one example—the practice of systematic personal knowledge management really came into vogue during the Renaissance with the emergence of commonplace books.[205] In 1865, Enlightenment philosopher John Locke wrote a treatise on how to record and categorize materials such as proverbs, speeches, ideas, and quotes. He advised people to keep their own records of information and store

---

205. *Ancient History Encyclopedia*, s.v. "Plutarch," by Mark Cartwright, updated February 25, 2016.

them in little books called commonplace books—a common place to store all knowledge.[206]

Locke, who himself had a home library of over 3,500 books, described a methodology of taxonomizing learned information into journals with easily-found sections, similar to the alphabetization of today's dictionaries. The idea was to create a supplemental memory, a failsafe for remembering important and useful facts. At the beginning of each commonplace book, Locke created an index showing where to find each bit of information inside the book.[207]

Commonplace books served as a personal database of information, and their use among highly influential, historical figures was widespread. Roman emperor Marcus Aurelius recorded his private thoughts about self-improvement and stoicism in one, which later became the *Meditations*.[208] Petrarch, who launched the study of literature during the Renaissance and resurfaced forgotten works like those of Cicero, used one.[209] Montaigne, father of the essay, used one to save his favorite sayings, quotes, and axioms.[210] Women, who were often excluded from higher education during the Renaissance, kept their own commonplace books to preserve learnings and educate themselves. Dorothy Wordsworth

206. Nicholas A Basbanes, *Every Book Its Reader: The Power of the Written Word to Stir the World*, (New York: Perennial, 2007).

207. "John Locke's Method for Common-Place Books (1685)," *The Public Domain Review*, accessed February 1, 2021.

208. Ryan Holiday, "How And Why To Keep A 'Commonplace Book,'" *Ryan Holiday* (blog), updated August 28, 2013.

209. *Ancient History Encyclopedia*, s.v. "Petrarch," by Mark Cartwright, updated October 22, 2020.

210. Holiday, "How And Why To Keep A 'Commonplace Book,'" 2013.

(William's sister, also a poet) kept one.[211] Thomas Jefferson, Napoleon, and Bill Gates also make the list.[212]

Even Kendrick Lamar, arguably the most influential rapper of the present day, is in on it.[213] As Lamar told record producer Rick Rubin:

> I have to make notes because a lot of my inspiration comes from meeting people or going outside the country or going around the corner of my old neighborhood and talking to a five-year-old little boy. And I have to remember these things. I have to write them down and then five or three months later, I have to find that same emotion that I felt when I was inspired by it, so I have to dig deep to see what triggered the idea… It comes back because I have key little words that make me realize the exact emotion which drew the inspiration.[214]

While commonplace books and physical zettelkastens are largely a thing of the past, their frameworks live on.

Some time ago, a close friend asked me where I stored all of the insights, facts, and quotes I referenced in my writing. When I stalled and began to describe odd notebooks and random documents, they turned me on to the idea of centralized knowledge. If everything was in one place and easily searchable, they said, it's not only easier to find but

---

211. Deborah Lynn Pfuntner, "Romantic Women Writers and Their Commonplace Books," *OakTrust*, Texas A&M University Libraries, 2016.

212. Holiday, "How And Why,'" 2013.

213. David Perell, "How to Cure Writer's Block," *David Perell* (blog), David Perell, accessed February 28, 2021.

214. *GQ*, "Kendrick Lamar Meets Rick Rubin and They Have an Epic Conversation," October 20, 2016, video, 49:47.

compounds on itself. This was the beginning of a deep and winding exploration into one of the systems I believe to be the most effective for cultivating exponential success: PKM.

Trapping the Flotsam

Personal knowledge management (PKM) is a catch-all term for the storage of valuable information in your life. Taking on many shapes and forms, PKM is a methodology of capturing, categorizing, and preserving external content as well as your own thoughts.

From inspiring quotes to the family budget to your ideas for a new business venture, having a net to trap the flotsam bobbing around in your brain captures valuable treasures and clears away distracting detritus. Typically, PKM targets the written word, but the information aggregated can also include images, audio, video, and other mediums like code.

Beyond just being a nice note-taking practice, however, personal knowledge management is an exceptionally powerful way to connect thoughts and ideas, cross-pollinating different areas of your world and leading to creative breakthroughs. It's a movement that has recently exploded as creators of all types and disciplines begin to discover its power.

These days, PKM is associated with note-taking software like Notion, Airtable, Evernote, Obsidian, or Roam Research, where people store and taxonomize digital information that they find useful, be it a Brené Brown quote or a broccoli casserole recipe. As we've seen, PKM has been around for centuries and is a lesser-known tactic of some of the greatest minds in history.

History lives on paper and stone. But the future, of course, is digital.

Where Genius Roams

After a long and varied career of filling sundry journals and notebooks with my thoughts, I finally began to upgrade my note-taking systems. I can't tell you how many times I've frantically searched through my physical notes for an important phone number or password, unable to click Control + F to easily find it.

So, I turned to the dark side. I went digital.

The PKM tool Roam Research became my drug of choice. Based off the zettelkasten, Roam operates as a tool for networked thought. Information is stored in nodes, or hyperlinked words, that connect to one another, not unlike a customized Wikipedia page.

Most of the stories in this book, in fact, were curated over time and collected in my Roam database. This chapter lived under a node tagged PKM. Under this umbrella, every other node that mentioned or was related to PKM was linked and easily accessible. The information on John Locke and the Kendrick Lamar quote from earlier in this chapter both had the tag, allowing me to easily retrieve and combine them into a cohesive narrative. A Roam database can be viewed as both a document and interactive graph, and my graph shows Kendrick and Locke connected in a web with lines to the PKM concept, which in turn is connected with a thousand other things. As I add to the database, tagging and connecting and intertwining seemingly-unrelated concepts like Enlightenment philosophers and rappers, the graph spiders outward and common threads and ideas start to emerge. Roam, like several of the PKM software companies in the budding knowledge management space, allows you to see your brain visually. The power of these current technologies is still niche, but quickly growing and gaining followings online as people begin to understand the incredible compounding effects they have on knowledge. The goal of Roam is not just note-taking, founder Connor White-Sullivan said; it's to collaborate with your future and past selves and allow your knowledge to compound.[215]

A system that definitively compounds your most valuable resource, your knowledge, is one of the hidden levers we've been looking for.

Author Steven Johnson recalls his experience of using a different digital PKM system to help him with his writing. "Private serendipity can be cultivated by technology... For more than a decade now, I have been curating a private digital archive of quotes that I've found intriguing, my twenty-first-century version of the commonplace book," he said.

When he connected two completely different stories, one about calcium in bone structure and one on London's sewer system in his book, Johnson wrote, "I'm not at all confident that I would have made the initial connection [between the stories] without the help of the software. The idea was a true collaboration, two very different kinds of intelligence playing off of one another... It lingered there for years in

215. Mark Traphagen, "How and Why I Launched Roam: Conor White-Sullivan on 20 Minute VC Podcast," Roam Tips, May 9, 2020.

the software's primordial soup, a slow hunch waiting for its connection."[216]

Building off earlier knowledge, whether your own or discovered by others, allows us to make connections and draw parallels to ideas. Making connections is the bedrock of creativity, and creating a system to facilitate it, particularly with technology, is a force multiplier that far exceeds the power of our own brains.

Shoulders of Giants

The basis of this theory is that what is recorded can be repurposed, repackaged, and remembered.

Humans are positively inundated with information. For almost every waking hour of our lives, we're bombarded with facts, theories, opinions, commercials, plotlines, chatter, and noise. Social media, movies, music, conversations, web browsing, reading, and even our own brain pelts us relentlessly with content to consume.

If you've ever tried meditating, you know how hard it is to shut off the monologues and diatribes within our own brains. A study at UC San Diego showed that Americans cumulatively consume information for about 1.3 trillion hours per year—which equates to an average of almost twelve hours per person per day—and the study only measured information that people consume *outside of work*.[217] As it were, the gray goo inside our skulls can only hold about seven pieces of

---

216. Steven Johnson, *Where Good Ideas Come From: The Natural History of Innovation*, (New York: Riverhead Books, 2011) 113-115.

217. Roger Bohn and James Short, "Measuring Consumer Information," *International Journal of Communication* 6 (2012): 980-1000.

information in short-term memory at once. Ipso facto, we forget almost all of this information about as quickly as we receive it.[218]

Can you recall the quote from the start of this chapter? It's likely that you'll have some vague sense of the message without being able to repeat it word-for-word; most of the information has already been lost. What's the point of learning information if we're just pouring water into a leaky bucket? How do we ensure our time spent accruing knowledge isn't just a zero-sum game? We must preserve knowledge outside of our own brains.

In Jonathan Swift's 1721 "A Letter of Advice to a Young Poet," Swift remarked that commonplace books were necessary for creators because, "Great wits have short memories."[219] Poets, but also doctors, mathematicians, musicians, teachers, and knowledge workers of all varieties benefit greatly from keeping a centralized database of knowledge.

As much as we'd like to think that we can create and learn and imagine all on our own, we're actually always borrowing from others. All creative work stems from inspiration, be it a sunset, a feeling, or a song. Pretty much everything that has ever been thought or created in some way piggybacks on existing work. Nothing is really, truly original.

Filmmaker Kirby Ferguson explores this topic in his documentary series, *Everything is a Remix*. From Bob Dylan songs that borrow lyrics from earlier music to *Star Wars* scenes that are filmed shot-for-shot the same as other movies,

---

218. Lauren Schenkman, "In the Brain, Seven Is a Magic Number," *Phys.org*, Phys.org, updated November 23, 2009.

219. Sir Philip Sidney, *English Essays*, Vol. 27, 51 vols, (The Harvard Classics. New York: Bartleby.com, 2001).

Ferguson unpacks how a significant portion of the media we love can be traced back to earlier content.[220]

Much of what we consider innovative is built on existing ground. However, this isn't necessarily a bad thing. Goethe said, "If you see a great master, you will always find that he used what was good in his predecessors, and that it was this which made him great."[221] So long as we remember and preserve it, we can build upon masterpieces that came before and make them *even better*.

Even Henry Ford stood on the shoulders of giants. Regarding the creation of the automobile, Ford said, "I invented nothing new. I simply assembled the discoveries of other men behind whom were centuries of work."[222] Certainly, innovation is built on the groundwork of other inventions, but the important part is knowing about them. Had Ford never learned about the automobile or the assembly line (neither of which he invented), and somehow stored this information for later retrieval, the Ford Motor Company wouldn't have come to fruition.

Storage is key. We cannot build upon that which we don't remember.

Exponential returns stem from having a cohesive place to store information. The mathematician with volumes full of calculations can reference and build upon them; The parent with an address book full of phone numbers will have an easier time finding a babysitter. If you have a repository to collect data, it will continue to grow and add more depth and

220. *Kirby Ferguson*, "Everything is a Remix Remastered (2015 HD)." May 16, 2016, video, 37:30.

221. Johann Peter Eckermann, *Conversations with Goethe*, (New York, NY: Ungar, 1946).

222. *Ferguson*, "Everything," 2016.

breadth to your endeavors, accelerating them exponentially as the database grows.

The How

We're not all in the business of creating handwritten, indexed volumes of every thought and whim that crosses our minds. That would be inefficient and cumbersome, not to mention impractical. Conversely, software databases aren't everyone's jam, either. There are better and worse ways to chronicle information, however, and also some good rules of thumb to guide your personal system creation.

Consider this: You're browsing the aisles of the grocery store when a new business idea strikes you like a slap to the face: 3 percent milk. It's edgy, it's new, it's bound to have huge demand from the farm-to-table and tech bro crowd alike. The business plan is already unfolding in your head. Markets, supply chain, distribution. The only question left is: Where do you write this down? You dig your phone out of your back pocket and your thumb freezes. Should you make a voice note? Open a Google Doc? Text your mom?

Productivity guru, Tiago Forte, has identified four qualifications for appropriate personal knowledge management systems, which he teaches in his PKM course, *Building a Second Brain*.[223]

According to Forte, the first quality in a good PKM system is durability. The information you record should be backed up automatically somehow, to a computer, to the cloud, or

---

223. *Tiago Forte,* "Building a Second Brain: Capturing, Organizing, and Sharing Knowledge Using Digital Notes," March 10, 2019, video, 44:13.

ideally, both. If you must write on paper, don't store it near the fireplace. There's no use in saving something if it can be easily lost.

Second, find a method that can capture different kinds of inputs: text, audio, video. The best PKM system should be a repository for all of the valuable information you want to save, unencumbered by the format.

Third, consider transparency. Information should be shown visually. You should be able to see and easily sort through your data and not have to dig through folder after folder to find what you want. You want to be able to efficiently make connections between various entries, and it's helpful to see it all in one place. The magic happens when you can find commonalities between information that isn't segmented into silos.

Finally, and perhaps most importantly, centralization: Everything must be stored in the same place. While it's all fun and games to have a personal library of notebooks of all sizes and shapes, it's clunky and disorganized. Pick one book, software, wall of a cave, whatever, and stick to it.

In communication theory, Marshall McLuhan's "the medium is the message" adage has lasted almost fifty years.[224] In many cases, the method something is communicated through is as important as the content communicated. For example, an audio file carries entirely different metadata from a handwritten note. In the former, tone of voice, tempo, and filler words convey a lot of information to the listener. In the latter, words may be chosen more carefully and it's easier to find information quickly.

---

224. Marshall McLuhan and Lewis H Lapham, *Understanding Media: The Extensions of Man*, (Berkeley, CA: Gingko Press, 2015).

Some people choose accessibility as their primary metric for picking a PKM system. My Grandpa Penny used to carry around tiny pocket notebooks everywhere he went. He always kept one in the breast pocket of his button-down shirts. Each evening, he would fill in details about his day. He may have met up with friends to go skiing. Maybe he did his taxes or went to the hardware store. I found a collection of these little notebooks just before his passing, when I was about nineteen. I remember touching all of their little leather covers and feeling impressed by his commitment to keeping them up all those years. His system worked for him, and he found it a great way to catalogue his life, leaving the breadcrumbs behind for his grandchildren to uncover.

I, too, am a big fan of having a paper, hard copy of a notebook. I take great solace in being able to fill the pages of a classic Moleskine unlined notebook with my thoughts and doodles. Physical notebooks are useful for short notes that I may later choose to input into my digital PKM system, and also great places for to-do lists. There's something so much more satisfying about manually crossing off a task with a pen. While digital PKM systems have durability and searchability built-in, the most important part is finding a method you'll stick with.

It's not hard to begin a PKM practice. Whenever a quote, fun fact, or interesting idea catches your eye, collect it. Find a medium that works for you. Begin to compile any notebooks or knowledge receptacles you already use into one place. Dedicated knowledge workers add to their commonplace books, knowledge software, or other PKM systems daily, detailing their learnings from every book, podcast, and conversation they have. This kind of enthusiasm may grow over time but start small. Commitment to the practice over the long run is how PKM turns from a fun little habit into a serious pathway to success.

Take note that PKM is not the same thing as journaling. Journals and diaries are inherently chronological, self-referential, and often written in a stream-of-consciousness format. The information isn't really meant to be useful or tactical, and journaled information tends to all morph together into a kind of soup. PKM is more like a charcuterie board; different elements like zettels and nodes are presented separately but can be paired to form unique and complementary combinations. PKM is a flavor of librarianship, a crisp cataloguing of thoughts, work, notes, data, and information from yourself and others. By keeping record of these things, you curate your own thought-space.

PKM centers around the common language of ideas. As ideas accumulate, they can start to talk to one another. They can be combined, arranged, synthesized, contrasted, connected, and compared to form the basis of opinions, arguments, theses, and general knowledge. The intersection of these separate ingredients affords incredible possibilities.

Though PKM systems are inherently organized, they don't have to be devoid of personal interpretations and feelings. But unlike pure journaling, the information saved is segmented, like puzzle pieces. The less personal they are, the more you may be inclined to share them. And communal knowledge management might just be the biggest tool we have yet for compounding human knowledge.

The Hive Mind

Digital PKM systems afford opportunities for collaboration. Entire teams can contribute to note-taking software to compile learned information, and the effect is like building a web of one hundred brains in one place. This collective intelligence concept is what makes the internet such a valuable resource. From academic papers to baby animal pictures, we can search through everyone else's content to find the information we need.

Accessibility of information is what allows humans to make significant progress. Vannevar Bush, an American engineer who is considered by some to be the godfather of the digital age, wrote a famous essay in *The Atlantic* in 1945 detailing the importance of shared information.[225] According to Bush, Gregor Mendel's concept of genes and inherited genetics was lost for more than three decades because his works did not reach those who were capable of understanding them. Remember Pareto, who discovered the 80:20 rule? His insights were buried for several generations before they were re-discovered.

"This sort of catastrophe is undoubtedly being repeated all about us, as truly significant attainments become lost in the mass of the inconsequential," Bush said. His article argues for the mechanization of records, or in today's terms, digitization, to allow people to easily access and build on one another's information.

Indeed, the hive-mind of collective, ongoing knowledge is largely what separates humans from the animal kingdom. Leveraging this power is key. While ants can collectively

---

225. Vannevar Bush, "As We May Think," *The Atlantic*, The Atlantic, July 1945.

build impressive structures and communicate information with one another, no single ant has an epiphany where they construct a pulley or lever to aid in their projects. If they did, they still couldn't effectively share the knowledge with others. Humans have both abilities: the power to innovate individually and the power to communicate ideas on a mass scale. The most important communication, however, is between the ideas themselves. The more we can make long-distance connections between different data points, which we'll discuss more in chapter twelve, the better our ideas will become. Creating a method for synthesizing so much information is incredibly powerful. As biologist E. O. Wilson "the father of biodiversity" wrote, "We are drowning in information, while starving for wisdom. The world henceforth will be run by synthesizers, people able to put together the right information at the right time, think critically about it, and make important choices wisely."[226]

Effective personal knowledge management is a force multiplier for synthesizing information, allowing for exponential gains in ideation, learning, and creative output. Whether you've got a zettelkasten on paper notecards or a digital database as your PKM system, the future knowledge is undoubtedly going to lie somewhere in the framework of networked thought. Developing a PKM practice is an Archimedes lever that will only expand and compound as information democratizes even further, lifting you even closer toward your moonshot goal.

---

226. E. O. Wilson, *Consilience: The Unity of Knowledge*, (New York, Knopf, 1998).

CHAPTER 11

MENTAL MODELS

Michelangelo was asked by the Pope about the secret
of his genius, particularly how he carved the statue of
David, largely considered the masterpiece of all masterpieces. His answer was: "It's simple. I just remove
everything that is not David."

—NASSIM TALEB

Via Negativa

Let us operate under the assumption that you want to change
your life for the better. Upon your first Google search of
the topic, you'll likely run into a great deal of noise about
building a better exercise routine, trying a miracle drug, psy-
chedelic, superfood, or adding in sundry daily practices to
increase well-being and happiness.

But what if the solution was actually to *do less?*

The solution for millions of religious devouts going back
millennia was to purify and clarify their lives by utilizing

via negativa, a system of adding by removing. *Via negativa* is Latin for "the negative path." In ancient Christian theological works, via negativa was a methodology for describing God, or ultimate perfection, by describing what God was not.[227] Instead of describing God in the affirmative ("God is love, God is light"), the apophatic theory holds that the Divine is limitless, boundless, nameless, and invisible. The idea is that humans do not have the ability to encapsulate the true essence of the Divine and must instead refer to it in the negative.

In other words, we don't understand God, so must instead describe what s/he isn't.

Via negativa has long been a method for gravitating toward perfection. Around the globe, nuns, monks, prophets, and other devouts separate themselves from society and worldly pleasures, removing distractions and vices, to get closer to their deities.

But via negativa isn't just for monks. Leaders of the minimalist movement like Marie Kondo and podcast hosts The Minimalists also encourage their followers to adopt a "less is more" strategy. While I'm not going to tell you how to tidy up your armoire or set fire to anything that doesn't immediately spark joy, we'll explore how using this mindset can act as a force-multiplier. By knowing what to leave behind, we clarify the way forward and create space for exponential success.

When we're young, we hold freedom of choice, options, opportunity, and physical possessions in high priority. We want to choose where to live, what kind of job to have, who to spend time with, and what to own. As we grow older, many of us adjust our definition of freedom to value having less. Naval Ravikant sums it up beautifully:

---

227. *Encyclopedia of Religion*, s.v. "Via Negativa," accessed January 12, 2021.

My old definition was *freedom to*. Freedom to do anything I want. Freedom to do whatever I feel like, whenever I feel like. Now, the freedom I'm looking for is internal freedom. It's *freedom from*. Freedom from reaction. Freedom from feeling angry. Freedom from being sad. Freedom from being forced to do things.[228]

Freedom from is a form of via negativa. Over time, the removal of distractions and irritants becomes more important than the addition of diversions. As we mature, we begin to look forward to going on vacations, not because of the ziplining and jet skiing and holiday activities, but to finally turn off our phones and ignore our daily responsibilities.

Practicing via negativa not only removes distractions but distills your work down into the most important pieces, allowing you to dive deep and become an expert in your category of choice.

Take cooking, for example. Some of the best restaurants in the world make incredibly simple dishes. They know that, though it can be even more challenging to create a masterpiece from fewer ingredients, simplicity can showcase the superior quality of the food and highlight the skill of the chef. Whereas McDonald's french fries have nineteen ingredients, Michelin star petite frites might have three or four, used sparingly.[229]

All-star chefs operate under the golden rule of making food: it's far better to under-season a dish and be able to add more in than to try and remedy an over-seasoned meal.

---

228. Nat Eliason and Neil Soni, "Seek Wealth, Not Money or Status. The Almanack of Naval Ravikant by Eric Jorgenson," *Made You Think Podcast*, Made You Think Podcast, October 26, 2020.

229. Roberto Ferdman. "There Are 19 Ingredients in McDonald's French Fries." *The Washington Post*. WP Company, updated April 26, 2019.

Mirazur, rated the best restaurant in the world in 2019, is predicated on simplicity. Head chef Mauro Colagreco sources most of the food from the garden at the base of the restaurant, picking the vegetables just hours before the dinner service.[230] His plates are beautiful, elegant, and simple. One recipe is titled simply, "Green" and features green things from his garden. Another is "Green Beans, Cherries, and Pistachio" which looks exactly as the title would indicate. Colagreco knows that delectable food isn't necessarily about what you add in but what you can take away. Stripping down to the elementals can produce extraordinary results.

Anthony Bourdain said, "Good food is very often, even most often, simple food."[231] The lesson: Start basic and master it before complicating things. In a moonshot mission, removing extra weight can be just as critical as adding extra thrust. Using via negativa to remove things from your life may be the exact key you need to make a quantum leap forward. Whether it's a toxic relationship, an unfulfilling job, poor eating habits, a social media addiction, or a negative mindset, consider taking stock of what you might choose to lose.

As Nassim Taleb said, "It is the negative that's used by the pros, those selected by evolution: Chess Grandmasters usually win by not losing; people become rich by not going bust (particularly when others do); religions are mostly about interdicts; the learning of life is about what to avoid."[232]

---

230. "Mirazur" The World's 50 Best Restaurants, William Reed Business Media, accessed January 24, 2021.
231. Maya Kachroo-Levine, "Anthony Bourdain Quotes That Will Inspire You to Travel More, Eat Better, and Enjoy Life," *Travel + Leisure*, Meredith Corporation, updated February 5, 2019.
232. "A Wonderfully Simple Heuristic to Recognize Charlatans," *Farnam Street* (blog), Farnam Street, updated November 12, 2019.

Billionaire investor Charlie Munger also echoed this sentiment. "It is remarkable how much long-term advantage people like us have gotten by trying to be consistently not stupid instead of trying to be very intelligent."[233]

So, what might we choose to eliminate in order to launch ourselves forward? Let's start with the toughest thing of all: other people.

Dunbar's Number

Via negativa can feel easier when we recognize that everything is finite.

How many people do you consider close friends? How about good friends? Acquaintances? Research suggests that we have a limited number of slots for people in each category.

In the 1990s, British anthropologist Robin Dunbar came across his now-famous measurement for relationships almost by accident. Dunbar was studying the grooming habits of primates when he happened to come across data that linked brain size of primates to the size of the social groups they congregated in.[234]

Dunbar discovered there was a direct correlation between the size of the neocortex (the part of the brain responsible for perception, language, and decision-making) and the size of the group the monkey congregated in. Consistently, the larger the group, the larger that piece of the brain was. In reverse, Dunbar realized that in reverse, this information

233. "Charlie Munger: The Power of Not Making Stupid Decisions," *CNBC MakeIt*, CNBC, updated August 4, 2017.
234. Maria Konnikova, "The Limits of Friendship," *The New Yorker*, Condé Nast, October 7, 2014.

meant ideal social group size could be predicted from the dimensions of the brain.

Humans are also primates, and Dunbar grew curious about the implications of this research. "We also had humans in our data set so it occurred to me to look to see what size group that relationship might predict for humans," he said.[235] How many people are humans supposed to know and spend time with? Is the number small, like the nuclear family, or huge, like the size of the cities we congregate in?

By doing the math, Dunbar came up with a number of people that the average human brain considered part of its social group. Remarkably, the number he came up with was almost exactly the same as the average group size of modern hunter-gatherer societies. It's also nearly identical to the number of guests at an average wedding: about 150 people.[236]

This number is what we can comfortably call casual friends. Very social people will have slightly more and less social people will have fewer, but the 150 people we can carry in our brains tends to break down into categories by a factor of three. The number of close friends the average human has is usually around fifty people. These friends are the type you'd invite to a group dinner. Beyond that, we each have about fifteen people we trust dearly and five friends or family members we might share the most intimate parts of our lives with. The rest of the 150 are casual friends or acquaintances.[237]

Because many people have several hundred or thousand connections on social media, it is surprising to learn that only 150 people really make the cut in the *actual friends* list our

235. Ibid.
236. Maddy Sims, "This Is the Average Wedding Guest List Size in the U.S.," Theknot.com, The Knot, updated October 1, 2019.
237. Konnikova, "The Limits of Friendship"

brains carry around. With such limited space, particularly in our closest social circles, via negativa can be an important metric for removing the bad apples from the batch.

Our best and most interesting friends will naturally work their way into our closest circles if they make us happy. It's much harder to let go of long-term sentimental friendships that are already in our bubbles but no longer serve us. Still, our time is the most precious thing we have, so it's worth taking a second look.

Author of the popular explainer blog "Wait But Why," Tim Urban breaks down the limited room in our life for the things we love in his illustrated essay "The Tail End." After calculating the likely number of days he had left in his life, Urban realized he had a finite amount of time before he died to experience certain things. "I'm thirty-four, so let's be super optimistic and say I'll be hanging around drawing stick figures until I'm ninety. If so, I have a little under sixty winters left," he writes.[238] Urban estimates he'll see about nine more presidential elections, go to twenty more Red Sox games, and eat pizza maybe seven hundred more times, at his current rate of once a month, before he kicks the bucket.

Reading about five books a year for fun, he'll only bag about three hundred more books in his lifetime. "I'll sign off for eternity without knowing what goes on in all the rest," he said. It makes you think twice about picking up an Ayn Rand if you know your total is ticking down.

The most powerful part of Urban's essay comes when he discusses the hours he has left with his parents. Urban realizes that by the time he graduated high school, he'd already

---

238. Tim Urban, "The Tail End," Web log. *Wait But Why* (blog), Wait But Why, December 11, 2015.

spent 93 percent of his total time with his parents. "I'm now enjoying the last 5 percent of that time," he says. "We're in the tail end."[239]

Knowing this, Urban now spends time with family more mindfully. If there was a debate whether to spend an evening with acquaintances or whether to kick back with Mom and Dad, his choice has already been made.

What can be measured can be managed. If you recognize you have a limited amount of hours left in your life, will you spend it with the people you care about most? Will you ditch the people who drag you down, say no to the invites you don't really want to say yes to, and be more selective about what you read and watch?

Minimizing the number of people in our inner circle is correlated with overall well-being. Psychologist Tim Kasser looked at the difference between *popularity* (the drive to be liked by a wide range of people) and *affinity* (the desire to deepen relationships). People who strived for popularity were found to be less happy, less healthy, and use more drugs than people who desired affinity. People in the affinity camp were happier and healthier overall, suggesting that deeper friendships are more important than having many to choose from.[240]

With a mere 150 slots for friends and family in our lives, the most important people are the top twenty. While adding in better friends can always slightly improve your well-being, removing the bad egg from the carton ensures you don't spoil the rest. Via negativa.

Becoming extremely selective about your social group is perhaps one of the biggest force-multipliers to success.

---

239. Ibid.

240. Tony Crabbe, "Why We're Better Off with Fewer Friends," *Quartz*, Quartz Media, October 2, 2015.

Research shows that toxic relationships are antigens to well-being. They have been shown to significantly impact the body, from slowing wound healing to causing fatal heart conditions.[241, 242] They also have an enormous impact on stress and can quickly leach time and energy away from your moonshot ambitions.

As they say, keep your good friends close and leave your enemies behind when you make it to the moon.

First Principles Thinking

Via negativa can also be applied to our thoughts. Bruce Lee said, "It's not the daily increase but the decrease. Hack away at the unessential."[243]

We can apply this back-to-basics mentality to our reasoning abilities as well as relationships. Just as simmering last night's cabernet down into a red wine reduction removes dilution in the liquid, simplifying our thinking processes strips away unnecessary information. Boiling down information to the core components is a key factor of smart decision-making. In mathematics, core beliefs are referred to as axioms or postulates. Physics and other theoretical sciences refer to them as *ab initio*, Latin for "from the beginning." Another term for this is reasoning from first principles, and it's a great place to start when solving problems.

---

241. Janice K. Kiecolt-Glaser, et al., "Hostile Marital Interactions, Proinflammatory Cytokine Production, and Wound Healing," *Arch Gen Psychiatry* 61, no. 12 (December 2005).

242. Mary Kyle, "Impact of Toxic Relationships on Heart Health," *EmpowHER*. Her Inc, updated February 25, 2019.

243. "#52 Hack Away the Unessentials," Bruce Lee, Bruce Lee Enterprises, updated June 29, 2017.

First principles thinking was first described by Aristotle in *The Metaphysics*. When studying philosophy, Aristotle attempted to first examine individual components of thought, or as he put it, "the first basis from which a thing is known."[244]

Now, Aristotle and others got their pantaloons all in a bundle about *unmoved movers* and where the first energy in the universe came from, but for everyday purposes, first principles thinking is a lot like the via negativa of thought. Thinking from first principles requires removing all unnecessary assumptions and knowledge, and it can be a great place to jumpstart creative thinking.

Tim Urban categorizes creators into two different categories: cooks and chefs.[245] Cooks work from recipes. They recreate already-made ideas, like pizzas, burgers, or tomato soups. Regardless of if they follow the recipe to a T or add in their own flair, their starting point already existed. Chefs, the true creators, begin from basic ingredients. They create concoctions from scratch that the world has never seen before, often optimizing to get the maximum amount of flavor out of their chosen building blocks.

The difference between chefs and cooks, musicians and cover artists, painters and curators, is that the true creators operate from first principles. They create from scratch, making original, beautiful, and powerful things, and as a result, they can usually make their mark on the world.

Urban writes, "For cooks, even the more innovative kind, there's almost always a ceiling on the size of the splash they can make in the world, unless there's some serious luck

---

244. James Clear, "First Principles: Elon Musk on the Power of Thinking for Yourself," *James Clear* (blog), updated February 3, 2020.

245. Tim Urban, "The Cook and the Chef: Musk's Secret Sauce," *Wait But Why* (blog), Wait But Why, updated November 6, 2015.

involved. Chefs aren't guaranteed to do anything good, but when there's a little talent and a lot of persistence, they're almost certain to make a splash."[246]

Achieving exponential success means transitioning from flipping burgers to designing the next ingestible protein. Getting there requires a combination of removing people and things that detract from your mission and utilizing first principles thinking to identify your building blocks.

The most famous first principles thinker of late is Elon Musk. When he set his sights on flying humans to Mars, the first question he asked was: How do I get there? Step 1: buy a rocket. He calculated that the price of a US-built rocket was about $65 million, not counting launch and labor costs. Though he'd made some good money from his previous entrepreneurial endeavors (Zip2, X.com, PayPal), it was far more than even he could afford.[247]

Searching for a different option, Musk asked two more deceivingly simple questions: *Where else can I get a rocket?* And *what could I use instead of a rocket?* Suddenly, he had a direction.

Between 2001 and 2002, Musk flew to Russia three times, hoping to score a deal on ICBMs, intercontinental ballistic missiles, that could be used as vehicles to get into outer space. The ICBMs were cheaper than the US-built rocket, but he was determined to find something even more affordable and customized to fit his mission.

Musk knew there had to be another way to achieve his goal, so he began to investigate the costs of the bare materials for a rocket. He told *Wired:*

---

246. Ibid.
247. Chris Anderson., "Elon Musk's Mission to Mars," *Wired*, Conde Nast, October 21, 2012.

I tend to approach things from a physics framework. And physics teaches you to reason from first principles rather than by analogy. So I said, OK, let's look at the first principles. What is a rocket made of? Aerospace-grade aluminum alloys, plus some titanium, copper, and carbon fiber. And then I asked, what is the value of those materials on the commodity market? It turned out that the materials cost of a rocket was around 2 percent of the typical price—which is a crazy ratio for a large mechanical product.[248]

And so, after simmering all of the information down into its most simple, logical pieces, Musk decided to build his own rocket. In 2008, SpaceX's *Falcon 1* rocket shot into orbit. The entire operation cost only about $7 million.

Reasoning from first principles removes the biases and assumptions that come from looking at the big picture. It can also pull back the curtain on unknowns.

Musk apparently has thought this way since childhood. "When I was a little kid, I was really scared of the dark," he said in an interview. "But then I came to understand, dark just means the absence of photons in the visible wavelength—400 to 700 nanometers. Then I thought, well, it's really silly to be afraid of a lack of photons. Then I wasn't afraid of the dark anymore after that."[249] Granted, Musk may operate on a more logical, even robotic, playing field than most, but his ability to reason from basic facts has allowed him to do incredible things.

Approaching reasoning, decision making, relationships,

248. Ibid.
249. *How Not To Give a Fuck*, "Elon Musk On Overcoming His First Fear," updated October 13, 2013, video, 0:32.

and planning with a via negativa mindset is a filter for noise. Identifying which information is truly necessary (first principles thinking) and which information does not serve the end goal of the process (via negativa) drastically clarifies the answers to important choices, giving you actionable steps toward achieving your moonshot.

Mental Models

Via negativa and first principles thinking are two of the most important mental models for moonshot goals, but there are a lot out there. Mental models act as guardrails for thinking, clarifying and simplifying information so you can make decisions faster and easier. They provide a toolbox to help you understand and navigate the world, acting as a filter to clarify the signal from the noise.

Mental models blend psychology with a whole host of other disciplines, like physics, statistics, and philosophy. Here are some other moonshot-relevant mental models to keep in mind:

Bayes' Rule (Also known as Bayesian Updating, Reasoning or Inference)[250]
- In short: updating one's beliefs with the appearance of new data
- Example:
  - The board game Guess Who? requires us to update our hypotheses as we ask questions. Players try and

---

250. *Big Think,* "Julia Galef: Think Rationally via Bayes' Rule," updated October 8, 2013, video, 3:22.

guess the cartoon character of their opponent, asking questions like, "Does your character wear glasses?" and eliminating options based on the answer. Though we learned to do this in childhood, adult humans often pick one belief system and refuse to change it, even as more information is acquired.

- Moonshot application:
  - Bayes' Rule helps us continually adapt and recognize that our belief systems are often more gray than black and white. When chasing a moonshot, try something, review outcomes, iterate, refine, and repeat.

Survivorship Bias

- In short: learning lessons only from successes, not failures.[251]
- Example:
  - During WWII, the US military wanted to armor their planes better and could only reinforce some areas or the planes would be too heavy. They decided to look at the planes returning from combat to see where the most bullet holes were and decided to armor those parts. Mathematician Abraham Wald stopped them. He realized they hadn't taken into account the planes that never made it back. The surfaces on the returning planes with the most bullet holes were actually the places a plane could be hit and still survive, the exact opposite areas the military should reinforce.
- Moonshot application:
  - Seek out failure stories and consider missing data.

---

251. Brendan Miller, "How 'Survivorship Bias' Can Cause You to Make Mistakes," *BBC Worklife*, BBC, August 28, 2020.

For every lottery winner, there are millions of losers, so one winner doesn't complete the picture.

Parkinson's Law

- In short: work expands to fill the time allotted.[252]
- Example
  - If you have an hour to cook dinner, you'll cook it in an hour. If you have twenty minutes, you'll still get it done. Creators of all types work according to their deadlines, knowingly or not. British historian and author Cyril Northcote Parkinson, to whom this law is attributed, uses the example of an elderly woman writing a postcard. Having nothing else to do with her day, it took her the whole day.
- Moonshot application:
  - Set short deadlines and meet them, or at least try to. Elon Musk almost always misses his deadlines, but he accomplishes things years faster than his competitors.
  - This also loosely relates to one of my favorite quotes of all time, by writer Anaïs Nin: "Life shrinks or expands in proportion to one's courage." The lesson: whether with time, courage, or any other life principle, we must choose the optimal container size.[253]

Just for Fun

- Here are a few of my favorite mental models and psychological tendencies, to be taken with a grain of salt:

---

252. Tiffanie Wen, "The 'Law' That Explains Why You Can't Get Anything Done," *BBC Worklife, BBC*, May 21, 2020.

253. "Thoughts On The Business Of Life," Forbes Quotes, *Forbes Magazine*, Accessed March 9, 2021.

- The Peter Principle: The tendency in most organizations for people to be promoted until they hit a level of incompetence, where they stay (satirical, but anecdotally observable).[254]
- The Lewis-Mogridge Position: When more roads are built, more traffic fills the roads. If it feels like you're always sitting in traffic, you are.[255]
- The Ballmer Peak: Some amount of alcohol increases cognitive performance (backed by one study, but largely anecdotal, named for Steve Ballmer of Microsoft).[256]

As somewhat of a minimalist myself, there are very few things I would encourage anyone to collect. Mental models are an exception. Using a personal knowledge management system, saving, storing, and regularly reviewing common mental models and human psychological biases is one of the most high-leverage activities moonshot-seekers can do with their time. For all their utility and power, human brains are still biased, shortsighted, affirmation-seeking, ego-riddled contraptions. The more we can stock our toolbox to mitigate these deficiencies, the better. *Via negativa* and first principles thinking are good starting points. From there, consider creating your own bento box of go-to mental models to dip into when the occasion arises.

254. Adam Hayes, "Peter Principle: What You Need to Know," *Investopedia*, Investopedia, updated August 28, 2020.
255. "Lewis-Mogridge Position," Academic Kids, accessed March 9, 2021.
256. Adrianne Jeffries, "Bottoms Up: The Ballmer Peak Is Real, Study Says," *Observer*, Observer, updated April 13, 2012.

CHAPTER 12

THE SECRETS OF SERENDIPITY

—

Most discoveries even today are a combination of serendipity and of searching.

—SIDDHARTHA MUKHERJEE

Strength in Differences

Combining similar things is easy, complementary, and intuitive. No one blinks an eye when they see three-cheese pizza on the menu or a bedroom painted both eggshell and alabaster white. Many of these neighborly pairings have already been done a thousand times.

Cohesion is comforting. True innovation and moonshot ideas, however, are often built when unlike things are combined. I remember doing a double-take when I learned that many football players take ballet to cross-train. While it may seem silly picturing three-hundred-pound men pliéing and sashaying across the floor, ballet is effective as a strength, balance, and flexibility practice in part because it works muscle groups in a completely different manner than typical football training usually does. The diversity of movement makes muscles more resistant to injury.

In the same vein, evolution favors the offspring of parents with diverse genes. Genetic diversity in humans creates positive genetic variations that help the species adapt and remain resistant to equally diverse pathogens. Parents with significantly different genetics have even been linked to having smarter children.[257] It would probably be much simpler for humans to reproduce asexually and split into two, like amoebas (goodbye, dating apps!), but the difficulty of doing so was evidently outweighed by the benefits of reproducing with two-parent organisms and mixing up the gene pool. Different things combined can create strength. Clearly, evolution didn't foresee what the dating climate would be like in the twenty-first century.

Just like pairing ballet with football creates well-rounded, injury-resistant athletes, combining unlike things can produce more favorable outcomes. In this chapter, we'll call the fortuitous pairing of unlike things "loose connections" and explore how their cultivation can increase both creativity and luck.

Loose Connections and Innovation

Some of the largest startups of today were borne out of seemingly adverse combinations. Take the car rental company Turo, for example, that brought private cars into the public space. Turo decided to combine the personal-rental

---

257. Philip Oldfield, "Diverse Parental Genes Lead to Taller, Smarter Children, Finds Extensive Study," *The Guardian*, Guardian News and Media, updated July 1, 2015.

phenomenon that Airbnb pioneered into the automobile space. Ten years ago, my jaw would have hit the floor if you told me people were routinely renting their personal cars out to complete strangers. Why would I ever entrust my vehicle to someone I didn't know?

As it turns out, this is the same reaction Silicon Valley investors had to Airbnb. In 2008, CEO and cofounder of the company, Brian Chesky, reached out to seven investors to raise funds for the company.[258] For $150,000, the investors could have bought 10 percent of the company. Five of the investors turned him down with short, curt emails. Two did not reply. Airbnb is now valued at over $100 billion.[259]

Turo, now nicknamed the Airbnb for cars, boasts over $500 million in funding and over fourteen million members who are renting out vehicles to one another.[260] The idea of sharing something personal with the public was once a taboo, distant thought, but innovative companies like Airbnb and Turo have capitalized on these unlike pairings to produce products and services that change the world. Adaptable people can quickly tap into these changes and benefit from them. A friend of mine bought a Series 4 BMW and paid off most of his car payments just by renting it through Turo.

Renting homes and personal vehicles is one thing, but what about combining mythical creatures and American history? Author Seth Grahame-Smith was in a bookstore when he noticed two distinctly different genres of books that

258. Brian Chesky, "7 Rejections," *Medium*, Medium, updated July 12, 2015.

259. Michael Goldstein, "Can Airbnb Continue To Grow After IPO Launches It to $100 Billion Valuation?" *Forbes, Forbes Magazine*, updated December 10, 2020.

260. Sophia Kunthara, "Turo Adds Another $30M To Series E," *Crunchbase News*, Crunchbase News, February 5, 2020.

had made it onto bestseller display tables: historical works and teen vampire novels. "Sort of shrewdly, from a cynical standpoint, I thought, 'Wouldn't it be great if you could combine these two things?" he said.[261]

Grahame-Smith went on to write *Abraham Lincoln, Vampire Hunter,* which reached the number four spot on the New York Times Bestseller list.[262] The novel later hit the silver screen as a Tim Burton-produced movie. Grahame-Smith's ability to combine two unlike things put him in a category of his own, a small pond the size of one, allowing him to stand apart from the crowd of both historical and vampire-focused authors.

The lesson? Don't be the best, be the only. Finding and combining distant data points sets you in a playing field of your own.

Scott Adams, author and creator of the prolific "Dilbert" cartoon capitalizes on this concept with his famous two-option career advice.[263] According to Adams, there are two primary methods of being successful.

- **Option 1:** Become the absolute best in the world at one specific thing. This technique is possible if you are extremely gifted in one area or pick an incredibly niche specialty, but is out of reach for the vast majority of us. While the payouts could be huge, it's risky and immensely challenging.

---

261. Michael Cieply, "Aside From the Vampires, Lincoln Film Seeks Accuracy," *The New York Times, The* New York Times, May 9, 2011.

262. "The New York Times Best Sellers," *The New York Times,* The New York Times Company, 2010.

263. Scott Adams, "Career Advice," The Dilbert Blog, updated July 20, 2007.

- **Option 2:** Become very good (Adams recommends in the top 25 percent) at two or more disparate disciplines. If you get a degree in engineering, Adams advises to double-major in something like art or biology. If you're an all-star chef, consider combining it with a niche skill like chemistry to bolster your ability to concoct dishes no one else can fathom. Adams credits his own success as a cartoon writer to combining his comedic abilities with his drawing skill. Not many funny people can draw, he noticed. Conversely, not many visual artists possessed the comedic gift, he said.

Option 1 is only open to a select few incredibly talented people. "The first strategy is difficult to the point of near impossibility," Adams writes. "Few people will ever play in the NBA or make a platinum album. I don't recommend anyone even try."[264] Making it to the top in a specific field also means eventually someone else will rise above you. Every number one chess champion is eventually beaten. Every Olympic gold-medalist eventually ages out of the sphere of competition. It's more compelling, then, to create a realm of your own with little or no competition.

Of both of these pathways to success, Option 2 is far more accessible. This option is an easier way to create a niche for yourself. It's also a more "antifragile" choice, as you have multiple skills that could carry you through a recession or career drought.

Even better than pairing two popular specialties is combining two or more *rarely combined* skills, say, computer science and communications or painting and cell biology.

---

264. Ibid.

In this case, it doesn't matter if you are the best if you are the only person in the world with a specific skill set. Having separate skills that complement one another acts as an Archimedes lever for success across the board. As far as combining painting and cell biology goes, some microbiologists do, in fact, paint with bacteria.[265] A hunch tells me they probably don't have a lot of competition.

"Capitalism rewards things that are both rare and valuable. You make yourself rare by combining two or more 'pretty goods' until no one else has your mix," Adams said. Pairing sui generis abilities not only sets you apart; it gives you the ability to draw inspiration from the confluence of the disciplines.

This is part of the genius of Leonardo da Vinci. Not only was da Vinci a gifted artist, but he drew inspiration from his experience in subjects like engineering, botany, and history to create some of the most important inventions and art the world has ever known. Many of the greatest creators in history fall into this category of generalized specialists—people who have a great deal of depth in one subject while also maintaining a medium level of competence in several other categories.[266]

The cherry on top of combining tangential skills is bringing your own, unique perspective to the table. Consider the career of Dr. Charles Limb, a surgeon who studies creativity. Limb researches the brain activity of jazz musicians as they improvise music in functional MRI machines.[267] An accomplished musician himself, Limb's two specialties have allowed

---

265. Rachel Hajar, M. D., "Painting with Bacteria," *Heart Views* 18, no. 3 (2017): 108.
266. "The Generalized Specialist: How Shakespeare, Da Vinci, and Kepler Excelled," *Farnam Street* (blog), updated March 1, 2020.
267. Charles Limb, "Your Brain on Improv," TED, TED Conferences, updated November 2010.

him to conduct research in an incredibly unique manner: musically collaborating with his patients.

Limb's primary inquiry was brain function during musical improvisation. He wanted to know what was happening inside the brain when people created music on the spot, and for improv to occur in a live setting, his study had to be participatory. As a result, he began improvising piano music back and forth with patients inside the fMRI machines at the National Institute of Health. Patients were outfitted with a small plastic keyboard that they could play, lying on their backs, inside the machine. Back in the control room, Limb played along with them, "trading fours," a common improvisation technique in jazz where each player plays four bars and riffs off the other. The machine measured areas of the patient's brain that "lit up," or had increased blood flow, during the improvisation periods. Limb compared the data to brain images of the patient playing memorized music.[268]

The unlikely pairing of participatory jazz and neuroimaging produced fascinating results. Limb found that the brain activates the same centers as both verbal communication and visualization when improvising music. "This whole notion that music is a language; maybe there's a neurologic basis to it after all, and we can see it when two musicians are having a musical conversation," he said. These conversations were made possible by Limb's disparate specialties: medicine and jazz. His ability to combine the two unlikely skills set him apart from scientists who had tried to study the same thing. As a result, his work produced incredible new insights into the brain that gives scientists a greater understanding of the roots of creativity.

---

268. Ibid.

"Most scientific studies of music are very dense, and when you go through them, it's very hard to recognize the music in them. In fact, they seem to be unmusical entirely and to miss the point of the music," Limb said. As both a musician and a scientist, Limb realized that these studies had to be approached by someone who understood both. "Why should scientists study creativity? Maybe we're not the right people to do it," he said.[269] But as both a musician and a scientist, Limb was able to re-engineer the problem and come at it from a different and unusual angle.

In either subtle or obvious ways, most of us have eclectic interests or talents. Identifying our own special blends is as easy as asking close friends, "What makes me weird?" or "What am I uncannily good at?" Exponential success often occurs when we maximize innate talents. Find what makes you weird or different and capitalize on it.

Beware the Dilettante

Combining two unlike skills certainly sets you apart, but what about combining more than two?

One method of preserving optionality in your work is increasing the number of niche skills you are good at. According to Angela Duckworth, author of *Grit*,

> In the study of excellence, what you find is that there are people who are not just 10 percent better than other people or 25 percent, they are *factors* better. They are true outliers. And one of the theories of human

---

269. Ibid.

excellence and the reason why the outliers are so out-side the distribution is because they are able to be in the top 10 percent of, say, *eight* different skills that you need to be successful in this overall endeavor.[270]

Eight skills? I can hardly name the eight planets, let alone specialize in eight different things. Some people are perhaps just extremely productive and will obsess over things until they gain mastery in them. If this is your niche, absolutely go for it. Beware, however, of dabbling. Uncommitted dabblers will fall into the master-of-none category, which detracts from exponential success. However, it's also a liability to become too specialized. As American journalist Henry Hazlitt wrote,

If he tries to be the Rounded Universal Man, like Leonardo da Vinci, or to take all knowledge for his province, like Francis Bacon, he is most likely to become a mere dilettante and dabbler. But if he becomes too specialized, he is apt to become narrow and lopsided, ignorant on every subject but his own, and perhaps dull and sterile even on that because he lacks perspective and vision and has missed the cross-fertilization of ideas that can come from knowing something of other subjects.[271]

Variety in expertise is helpful. But too much of a good thing can hurt you in the long run. Someone like Duckworth, whose overachievement is famous (she won a McArthur

270. Angela Duckworth, "What's the Downside to Being Goal-Oriented?" produced by Rebecca Lee Douglas, podcast audio, No Stupid Questions, Freakonomics, August 30, 2020.
271. "The Generalized Specialist," *Farnam Street* (blog), 2020.

genius grant and her resume reportedly spans fifteen pages), could probably master eight skills. For most of us, however, this is likely overkill. Specializing in two or three areas is probably enough to carve out a competition field of zero. Even better, adopting the generalized specialist mentality and going deep on a few select things but shallow on a wide range of topics will help you stay well-rounded.

Whether you have two or eight or twenty skills, curating a variety and a diverse set of inputs is also a key ingredient of serendipity and luck.

Serendipity

Beloved PBS painting instructor Bob Ross is perhaps best known for his assertion that, "We don't make mistakes, just happy little accidents." Ross believed that unintended brush strokes could turn into beautiful trees or mountains, a framework that helped him create beautiful painting after beautiful painting with fast, sure strokes. "Happy accidents" are a form of luck, as is serendipity. With careful curation, both can be created.

Serendipity is a perfect cocktail of determination and time. Anytime a serendipitous moment occurs, success spikes. These are the spurts of purest acceleration, the eureka moments where the locked door finally swings open to reveal the next stage of progress.

Loose connections encourage serendipity by opening multiple doors of possibility. Gaining expertise in two or more disconnected fields, say car mechanics and pasta making or sociology and horticulture, allows you to use one lens of expertise to look at the other, giving you a unique and exciting opportunity to discover what has been overlooked by others. Twitter is famous for creating serendipitous connections between people in unique niches. Seamus Blackley is one example. Known best for creating the Xbox, Blackley is also a self-proclaimed gastroegyptologist, combining his passions for both bread baking and ancient Egypt. In 2019, Blackley began to take an interest in bread yeasts collected from Egyptian pottery.[272] After baking his first loaf with questionably ancient yeast, he posted about it on Twitter. The enthusiasm was so huge, he set out to do it for real.

What do you get when you put a video game designer/physicist/gastroegyptologist, an archaeologist, and a biologist together? Carbohydrate magic.

Sharing his creation led Blackley to the serendipitous connection of the two people who could help him most in his niche endeavor: Dr. Serena Love, an archaeologist with a background in Egyptology, and Richard Bowman, a biologist at the University of Iowa. Though they were skeptical of his mission to bake a replica of ancient Egyptian sourdough bread, the three soon joined forces to make the mission happen. After countless hours of research and emailing people in her field, Dr. Love was able to secure access to ancient Egyptian pottery in museum archives. Once the artifacts became available, Bowman donned full-body protection, so as not to contaminate the specimen, and used non-invasive techniques to extract the ancient yeast from the clay surfaces.[273, 274]

---

272. Luke Fater, "How the Man Who Invented Xbox Baked a 4,500-Year-Old Egyptian Sourdough," *Atlas Obscura*, Atlas Obscura, updated April 2, 2020.

273. Ibid.

274. Jenny G. Zhang, "A Conversation with the Team That Made Bread with Ancient Egyptian Yeast," *Eater*, Eater, updated August 8, 2019.

Blackley, who has a degree in physics, claims his mathematical background was helpful in crafting the sourdough. "It's what your physics, or math, or engineering brain does with anything; you look at it, and you dissect it, and you want to find its purest part in its purest form … And so a lot of engineers and scientists end up making sourdough," he said.[275]

After many trials and errors, Blackley was able to revive the yeast and bake it into a sourdough loaf with the same ingredients ancient Egyptians likely used. His feat made headlines and created a buzz in the sourdough scene. No one else had been able to create a loaf using actual ancient yeast and ingredients that both looked edible and tasted delicious. "It produced a soft, super high, fluffy loaf of Einkorn and barley bread. Which, as any baker will tell you, is really impossible. Baking with ancient grains produces pucks. I've worked for years to be able to bake with Einkorn," he said.[276]

Blackley is still working with Love and Bowman on collecting the yeasts and perfecting the baking technique. They're even sequencing the genome of the yeast to get the purest form possible. Without the help of his serendipitous team of helpers, Blackley might still be a hobbyist tinkering with everyday yeast in his kitchen. Instead, he's leading the charge to revive a food that hasn't been seen in its intended form for thousands of years. Blackley says the re-discovered bread is so good it rivals whole-wheat bread. "That smell of brown sugar, the way it triggers something in your brain that's just really good. It was pretty exciting. I was very emotional late Sunday night, when [the first loaf] came out of the oven."[277]

275. Gastroegyptology (BREAD BAKING) with Seamus Blackley," Ologies, July 7, 2020.
276. Zhang, "A Conversation," 2019.
277. Ibid.

Blackley's loose connections, his niche interests in Egyptology, bread baking, and physics, laid the groundwork for serendipity. The final ingredient in his bread-baking success, of course, was simply luck.

Chance & Luck

While some elements of success are simply left up to chance, there are some excellent strategies to please the gods of luck. Loose connections are one of them. Blackley's odd talents culminated into a *perfect storm* of serendipity, one of the four kinds of luck identified by American neurologist James H. Austin.[278] While some forms of luck are completely random and can't be controlled, others can be induced by properly setting the stage.

The first category of luck Austin identified is blind luck. Austin calls this pure luck "Chance I." It happens without any prompting, like finding a $100 bill on the sidewalk, and nothing can influence or induce it. It occurs at random, like an act of God. Most of us probably have the same amount of this kind of luck in our lives.

The second type of luck is "Chance II," where a person has set outcomes in motion by pursuing a certain action. Just like Bob Ross' accidental brush strokes that become beautiful trees, Austin calls Chance II "happy accidents." Chance II is another name for the Kettering Principle, which states that being in a state of motion results in a higher likelihood of

---

278. James H. Austin, *Chase, Chance, and Creativity* (MIT Press, 2003), quoted in Marc Andreessen, "Luck and the Entrepreneur, Part 1: The Four Kinds of Luck," PM Archive, updated August 14, 2007.

collisions between people and ideas.[279] In other words, you won't accidentally create a happy little tree or even an artistic masterpiece if you never pick up a paint brush. A measure had to be taken to set everything into motion.

The first two types of luck can happen to anyone. The second two require effort and specialization. Austin believed specialists were more likely than amateurs to have profound strokes of luck in their work. The third type of luck he identified, Chance III, favors those with a foundation of knowledge who can recognize opportunities when they see them. Chance III occurs when luck meets preparation.[280] A specialist can spot once-in-a-career opportunities, or black swan events, where a generalist would miss them.

"The last kind of luck is the weirdest, hardest kind," Angellist's Naval Ravikant says.[281] The final category, Chance IV, "occurs when you behave in ways that are highly distinctive of you as a person," writes Austin.[282] Contributing factors include distinctive, eccentric hobbies and personal lifestyles.

"[Chance IV] is where you build a unique character, a unique brand, a unique mindset, where the luck finds you," Ravikant said. "For example, let's say that you're the best person in the world at deep sea underwater diving. You're known to take on deep sea underwater dives that nobody else will even attempt to dare. Then, by sheer luck, somebody finds a sunken treasure ship off the coast. They can't get it. Well, their luck just became your luck, because they're going to come to

279. Ibid.
280. Ibid.
281. Naval Ravikant, "Making Money Isn't About Luck," Naval, updated January 31, 2020.
282. Austin, *Chase, Chance, and Creativity,* 76.

you to get that treasure. You're going to get paid for it."[283]

The most elusive form of luck can be created by developing niche specializations. Fostering loose connections specifically tailored to your strengths, in other words, creates a perfect storm for Chance IV to step in and accelerate your moonshot.

Type of Luck	What It Looks Like	Influenced By	Also Known As
Chance I	Complete, random chance. Not triggered by anything.	Nothing	Blind Luck
Chance II	Happy accidents. Something was already set in motion, and the outcome is positive.	Action	The Kettering Principle
Chance III	Your past experience and preparedness allowed you to take advantage of something others would have missed.	Hard work and expertise	The Pasteur Principle
Chance IV	Individualized chance. Luck favors those who act according to who they are as a person. Very niche & specific.	Intuition and instinct	The Disraeli Principle

Blackley's success in creating ancient Egyptian bread came where many others failed because he combined many different varieties of chance to make it happen. Blackley used his science background to dive deeply into the first principles of

---

283. Ravikant, "Making Money," 2020.

bread making, experimenting with different kinds of grains until he found one that worked with the ancient yeast. Thousand-year-old yeast, Blackley discovered, won't grow with modern flour. It needs Emmer flour, a denser and more archaic grain, to be revived.[284] Blackley's ability to identify the right grain is likely an instance of Chance IV, a reflection of Blackley's extremely niche interest coupled with his unrelenting perseverance, coming together to produce a lucky break.

Additionally, Blackley discovered through tinkering that the yeast fermented the best at exactly 94° F, the average daytime temperature around the Nile. He estimates he baked around seventy-five loaves before constructing an in-ground oven in his backyard to mimic the ancient Egyptian technique. "If I hadn't spent so much time working on it, it would have been a wreck," Blackley said. "I would have been another one of those people posting a shitty, burned, flat loaf saying, 'Welp, I guess this is what the ancient Egyptians had to deal with!'" Instead, he describes the bread as being sweet and chewy, remarkably more pleasant than what people had previously believed ancient bread to be.[285] This is Chance III, using a foundation of baking and science knowledge to aid in the success of the final product.

Blackley also utilized Chance II, serendipity, by posting about his quest on Twitter, which led him to connect with the two specialists, Dr. Love and Bowman, who were able to secure for him the resources he needed. He was probably also aided by Chance I, that any yeast at all remained on the ancient Egyptian ceramics.

---

284. Fater, "How the Man," 2020.
285. Ibid.

Synthesizing

While luck is, of course, not guaranteed, there are several definitive steps you can take to invite it to the party. First, you must have a bias toward action. This is epitomized by hockey Hall of Famer Wayne Gretzky's famous assertion, "You miss 100 percent of the shots you don't take."[286] Hitting as many pucks as possible into the net during hockey practice or baking obscene amounts of bread are both ways to increase the likelihood of success.

Second, you must accumulate resources by gathering diverse sources of knowledge. Working cross-functionally with people of different disciplines or versing yourself in unrelated, niche areas allows different lenses to be placed over the same problem. This increases the probability of coming to uncommon and diverse solutions.

Third, you must fuse the diverse inputs together. Though acquiring varied inputs of knowledge can seem complex, even daunting, complexity isn't necessarily a bad thing. "A complex engine, for instance, not only has many separate components, each performing a different function, but also demonstrates a high sensitivity because each of the components is in touch with all of the others," said Mihaly Csikszentmihalyi.[287] Synthesizing diverse inputs, thus, is a third critical component to luck and serendipity. Using techniques like personal knowledge management and mental models to gather, combine, and integrate information allows it to be

---

286. Paul B. Brown, "'You Miss 100 Percent of the Shots You Don't Take,' You Need to Start Shooting at Your Goals," Forbes, Forbes Magazine, updated January 12, 2014.

287. Mihaly Csikszentmihalyi, *Flow: The Psychology of Optimal Experience.* (New York: Harper & Row, 1990) 41.

shuffled much like a Rubik's cube until the right combination is found. Pattern identification and identifying areas of overlap is the bedrock of creativity and innovation.

There is also an unintuitive ingredient to harnessing the power of luck and serendipity: empty space. Patterns tend to solidify during moments of rest and free association. Ironically, not doing anything may be a key component to creative breakthroughs, which may explain why boredom is suddenly *in vogue* in the tech community. Founders, thinkers, and tinkerers are finally realizing the power of unplugging, stepping away, and letting inspiration strike when it's ready.

Anagnorisis, the part in the play where a character goes from ignorance to knowledge (another concept brought to us by Aristotle), infamously arrives in moments where the character's mind has space to wander. The noise-silence-signal pattern is recognizable across disciplines. It's why good ideas come in dreams, on long runs, or during lazy days at the beach. The pieces come together when we step away from the stimulus and let our subconscious do the work. One of the most famous ways of encouraging anagnorisis is simply going for a walk.

Do As the Romans Do

Walking has been a technique used by great thinkers for centuries. Philosopher Friedrich Nietzsche once proclaimed that "all truly great thoughts are conceived while walking." Steve Jobs, Beethoven, Goethe, Thoreau, and Darwin were all fans of a good stroll to get the ideas flowing.[288]

---

288. Oliver Burkeman, "This Column Will Change Your Life: A Step in the Right Direction," *The Guardian*. Guardian News and Media, July 23, 2010.

Ambulatio, strolling about and thinking, was also a favorite pastime of ancient Romans. Pliny the Younger, an Ancient Roman magistrate and prolific writer, left detailed records of his days that were punctuated by walks at all hours, some solitary and some with fellow intellectuals.[289]

The Romans intuited what Stanford researchers later discovered: walking boosts creativity. A 2014 study by university researchers found that walking increases a person's creative output by an average of 60 percent.[290] According to the study, not only did people produce more ideas, their ideas were better: "People presented more ideas, and the ideas tapped each person's unique associative network, which led to an increase in novelty compared with other people's ideas," the study said.

Still, it doesn't suffice to say that we should all stroll around endlessly, hoping for our eureka moments to strike. The key is to introduce new knowledge or a thought-provoking conversation, and then let it marinate in the brain for a while, whether you go on a long walk or bake a cake. Try listening to a podcast and then doodling, walking, or meditating. With time, the mind sorts through the new information and sifts the wheat from the chaff.

Geek Out

What's next? You've added new information to your brain, formed loose connections between thoughts and people outside of your social circle, encouraged the deities of chance to

---

289. Ibid.
290. Marily Oppezzo and Daniel L. Schwartz, "Give Your Ideas Some Legs: The Positive Effect of Walking on Creative Thinking," *Journal of Experimental Psychology: Learning, Memory, and Cognition* 40, no. 4 (2014), 1142-52.

look favorably on your life, and now you're strolling everywhere you go. Things are in motion. Now, there's one last piece to the puzzle: Get weird.

The fifth and final helpful quality for boosting luck is being a curious, obsessed nerd. Geeking out about eccentric, random, or niche hobbies is a tried-and-true method of creating beautiful, useful, and breakthrough inventions. Passion, curiosity, and forward momentum set the stage for serendipity and luck. "An obsessive interest in a topic is both a proxy for ability and a substitute for determination," Paul Graham said.[291] In other words, taking a deep interest in something can be just as or more valuable than having expert talent or skill and being highly disciplined at pursuing it.

If you don't have a skill or peculiar interest just yet, don't worry. Take some time to expose yourself to new and different stimuli and see what grabs your attention. The Roam Research whitepaper encourages the pursuit of odd mental nodes:

> Just as humans are incapable of generating random numbers, we struggle to consciously generate random ideas, to the point where actively trying to think differently often seems to only further calcify existing patterns.

> Instead of attempting to brute-force creativity, the brain must be confronted with novel stimuli in order to reorganize its perception. Exposure to a certain amount of random "noise"—drugs, dreams,

---

291. Paul Graham, "The Bus Ticket Theory of Genius," Paul Graham, November 2019.

meditation, Tarot readings, mistakes—can jolt thoughts out of well-tracked grooves and into entirely new areas of idea-space. Typically these insights occur at the juncture of two or more seemingly unrelated fields, concepts, or images.[292]

Going down odd rabbit holes, joining special interest communities, and becoming obsessed with seemingly irrelevant things is a way to differentiate yourself from the crowd. Generalized specialists do best when one or more of their interests is completely out of left field.

"Chance favors the prepared mind," Louis Pasteur famously said.[293] The best way to be prepared is to take a deep and genuine interest in something, no matter how strange or obscure. Combine loose connections and serendipity with some empty space, and inspiration is soon to come knocking.

292. "Roam White Paper," Roam Research, accessed February 22, 2021.
293. "Thoughts On The Business Of Life," *Forbes*, Forbes Magazine, accessed February 28, 2021.

CHAPTER 13

CHAOS

A little bit of agitation gives resources to souls and what makes the species prosper isn't peace, but freedom.

—JEAN-JACQUES ROUSSEAU

The increase of disorder or entropy is what distinguishes the past from the future, giving a direction to time.

—STEPHEN HAWKING

Systems and tactics are a key aspect of Archimedean achievements, so it may surprise you to learn an unintuitive secret ingredient to exponential success: a little bit of chaos.

You see, humans are built to withstand and even benefit from a certain amount of randomness and uncertainty. We need it to advance progress. If we develop the tolerance and mindset to withstand it, we can actually learn to thrive just as much during times of chaos as times of peace.

Before we begin, let's explore chaos for a moment. According to the Merriam Webster dictionary, Chaos is "a state of things in which chance is supreme."[294] In other words, it is a place of possibility, of the unknown. It is the opposite of predictability. While slow, linear growth is predictable, exponential growth is often chaotic and unexpected. We can't typically predict the moment that a song like "Gangnam Style" is going to go from obscurity to virality. The music video from the previously unknown artist now sits at nearly four billion views on YouTube, something no one could probably have anticipated.[295] Exponential growth is slow, then sudden. The pivot point, or fulcrum, where the graph climbs from a slow curve to that dramatic, hockey-stick incline, is most often preceded by an injection of energy, of chaos.

A dose of the unknown is perhaps the "special sauce" of exponential growth. Learn how to cultivate and manage it, and you can lasso that rocket ship and ride it to the moon.

Dissipative Structures

Like it or not, we live in a chaotic world. Life is a steamroller, and evolution flattens any species or system that is too fragile to adapt. People who sustain success in the long-term learn to use this chaos to their advantage.

Once in a while, an individual bypasses the slow climb to exponential success and lands at the top in the blink of an eye. The life trajectory of a lottery winner is one example, if we're measuring success from a monetary perspective. The challenge

---

294. *Merriam-Webster*, s.v. "Chaos (n.)," accessed February 3, 2021.
295. *Officialpsy*, "PSY—GANGNAM STYLE(강남스타일) M/V," July 14, 2012, video, 4:12.

with such dramatic success is that it's unsustainable. If you don't do the work to get there, you won't last at the top. Lottery winner happiness, if graphed on a chart, would look somewhat like a dying person's last heartbeat on an EKG: a steep increase followed by a dip below the midline and eventual flatline. The kind of success we hope to achieve in this book isn't so volatile. It consistently increases over time. Despite some inevitable dips and bursts, the increase is sustained.

Ancient philosopher Heraclitus is known for his assertion that "Life is flux," often interpreted as "the only constant in life is change."[296] The best way to ensure you're on an upward trajectory is to actively use the chaos to your benefit.

The best examples of net-positive systems that have withstood the test of time are found in nature. Plants, for example, feed on the loose, random energy waves in the air: light. Nobel Laureate Ilya Prigogine crafted a theory around this called dissipative structures, or systems that harness energy that would have been lost to randomness. Plants are dissipative structures because they depend on this random, excess energy to thrive, and in turn, feed the whole animal kingdom.[297]

As humans, we get to choose whether to be dissipative structures or not. We can either wilt and shrink from the curveballs and hardships life throws at us, or we can metabolize them and turn them into something great. Both options include suffering; there's really no escaping that, I'm afraid. But a strategic first step in using chaos to our advantage comes in the form of systems.

---

296. *World History Encyclopedia.* s.v. "Heraclitus of Ephesus," by Joshua J. Mark, updated July 14, 2010.

297. Mihaly Csikszentmihalyi, *Flow: The Psychology of Optimal Experience,* (New York: Harper & Row, 1990), 201.

Cultivating Robust Systems

Ah, yes. This is the part of the book where we talk about systems. Bear with me, here. I'm not going to give you a ten-step program or a morning routine. Instead, we'll explore what happens when you-know-what hits the fan.

Our ideal selves all have the perfect systems built into their lives. Whether it's sending fifty emails a day to potential investors in our startup or reading machine learning and quantum mechanics books for three hours a day, we'd all love to be that super productive, imaginary person who follows our ideal mental routines. Sometimes we actually achieve it. We'll go for a jog two days in a row or use the Headspace app for an uninterrupted fifteen minutes of meditation and feel on top of the world. But then we'll fall off the bandwagon. Life gets in the way.

Certainly, following our ideal routines is easier in weeks when you aren't stressed, traveling, or feeling distracted by life events. But how often do you have a perfect week? If you're anything like me, it's rare to find a seven-day streak where absolutely nothing goes wrong and you can charge, uninterrupted, toward your moonshot goal. Despite my best intentions and the accountability systems I've put into place, I often find myself going off the rails and ignoring my to-do list when things get tough. This is a critical mistake.

It is, in fact, exponentially more important not to fall into a downward spiral than it is to increase your upside.

Let me explain. There's a tricky thing in math that our brains aren't very good at: calculating percentage gain and loss. We'll use an investing example, but don't get wigged out by the numbers. Let's say you start with $100 and suffer a 50 percent loss. You now have $50. Darn. Next, you make 50 percent back. Yay, you're back where you started! Not so fast. You actually only have $75 now. Making back half of $50 only adds $25 to your pile. Did you catch that? You'd have to experience a *higher percentage gain* to get back to your starting place. It's like you just got knocked down into a hole and there's quicksand on the way back up to the top. This principle operates in the reverse as well. If you start with $100 and make a 50 percent jump up to $150, it will only take a 33 percent drop to put you back where you started, at a single Benjamin in your pocket. In other words, that 33 percent loss is just as powerful as a 50 percent gain. Using chaos to build robust systems becomes increasingly important once you realize how hard it can be to recover from a loss.

Not to mention—experiencing losses is a total bummer. Behavioral economics teaches us that humans will go to greater lengths to avoid losses than to increase gains because losses cause us psychological pain. When people are faced with either a pizza that they have to take ingredients off of or blank pizza dough that they will add ingredients to, they'll remove far fewer tasty bites then they'll add.[298] We don't like to give away what we feel like we've already earned.

Removing sausage nibblets certainly counts as chaos in my book, so how does chaos actually increase exponential success? One significant upside is it encourages, or rather requires, us to build robust systems for good habits.

Habit guru James Clear writes about a college roommate who developed a mantra to help him train for baseball on

298. Irwin P Levin, et al., "A Tale of Two Pizzas: Building Up from a Basic Product versus Scaling Down from a Fully Loaded Product," *Marketing Letters* 13, no. 4 (November 2002): 335-44.

even the most difficult days: train for chaos. According to Clear, "'Train for chaos' was a simple way of saying, 'Don't tell me that the circumstances aren't ideal. Tell me that you're going to make it your responsibility to be better prepared next time.'"[299] In other words, build a system that is weatherized against the rain.

Chaos is inevitable. If you don't anticipate the chaos and constant change, you can't control your future. The hidden benefit of this foresight is that our systems grow stronger. Chaos forces us to build stronger systems, so they endure. We don't build our houses for sunny days; we build them for storms.

Creativity Through Antifragility

Building strong systems doesn't just mean they'll last longer. They also might be better and more creative overall.

Enter: author and statistician Nassim Taleb's concept of *antifragility*. As it turns out, some things in life actually suffer from homeostasis and thrive from adversity. Learn to become antifragile and you're as close as you can get to being invincible.

Some things in life are fragile, like porcelain teacups. Despite whatever measure of joy you would get out of the action, a porcelain teacup would not benefit from being thrown against a wall. Other things are antifragile and actually benefit from hardship. Hydra, the serpentine monster from Greek and Roman mythology, thrives when the chaos hits the proverbial fan: She grows two heads back for every head that is cut off. Some real-world examples of antifragility

---

299. James Clear, "How to Stick to Your Goals When Life Gets Crazy," *James Clear* (blog), updated February 4, 2019.

are our bones and muscles. Both get stronger from being put under the moderate stress of exercise and can atrophy or become brittle with disuse.

Fragile   **Robust**   **Antifragile**

While robust systems can withstand chaos, antifragile systems thrive on chaos. And since randomness and chaos are the only reliable things in life, the strongest systems learn to embrace and benefit from them. "[Nature] is aggressive in destroying and replacing, in selecting and reshuffling. When it comes to random events, 'robust' is certainly not good enough," Taleb says.[300] Becoming antifragile is the difference between tolerating the rain while training for baseball and intentionally training in the rain to get better at managing the slippery conditions.

So then we must move from avoiding and tolerating chaos to actively cultivating it. How does this occur?

On a small scale, it means simply doing something *different* than your normal routine. If you usually read biographies, pick up a sci-fi novel. If you always take the same route home from work, drive through a neighborhood you've never been to. The goal is to create a diverse set of inputs to your brain, grow comfortable with the uncomfortable, and help us rapidly adapt.

---

300. Nassim Nicholas Taleb, *Antifragile: Things That Gain from Disorder*, (New York: Random House, 2016), 9.

Often, however, we see this concept play out on a much larger scale. Two researchers at the Vienna University of Economics and Business noticed something interesting when they began researching entrepreneurs: immigrants to the US were almost twice as likely as native-born citizens to become entrepreneurs.[301] The immigrant entrepreneurs were also incredibly successful. In fact, 216 of the Fortune 500 companies in 2017 were founded by immigrants—that's 43 percent! Considering immigrants only make up about 13 percent of the population, the researchers wanted to know what made immigrants so disproportionately successful in the notoriously difficult entrepreneurial space.[302]

They found multiple theories to explain the phenomenon. Studies suggest that entrepreneurial individuals are more likely to immigrate and/or may choose self-employment due to discrimination in labor markets.[303] But these researchers found something else.

Immigrants, it turns out, are primed for opportunity recognition. Cross-cultural experience helps people spot emerging markets and find holes in existing markets. They also partake in knowledge arbitrage, borrowing ideas from one place and implanting them somewhere new. Red Bull Energy Drink founder Dietrich Mateschitz did this when he took a trip to Thailand and saw truck drivers and construction workers drinking a cheap energy drink.[304] He decided to license the

---

301. Peter Vandor and Nikolaus Franke, "Why Are Immigrants More Entrepreneurial?" *Harvard Business Review*, Harvard Business Publishing, updated October 27, 2016.

302. Ana Campoy, "216 Companies on the Fortune 500 Were Founded by Immigrants or Their Children," *Quartz*, Quartz Media, updated December 9, 2017.

303. Vandor and Franke, "Why," 2016.

304. Ibid.

product and promote it in the Austrian clubbing scene, to great success. Both opportunity recognition and knowledge arbitrage tie back to loose connections and personal knowledge management. Having diverse inputs creates creative outputs. Innovative ideas don't happen in a vacuum. They are inspired by a mishmash of inputs and typically involve combining two or more highly tangential data points, like living in two or more countries. These data points are collected from diverse experiences, both good and bad. Like Steve Jobs said,

> Creativity is just connecting things... A lot of people in our industry haven't had very diverse experiences. So they don't have enough dots to connect, and they end up with very linear solutions without a broad perspective on the problem. The broader one's understanding of the human experience, the better design we will have.[305]

Not only did Jobs recognize that linear progress is, in fact, underwhelming, he advocated for diverse, hard, and even weird life experience. Jobs was no stranger to encounters with LSD or trekking around in a loincloth in India and was partial to eating strange diets, like one fruit or vegetable at a time for weeks.[306] Did these hard experiences help him become successful? Perhaps—he somehow developed a remarkably thick skin to the tumultuous politics of Silicon Valley and found success even after being ousted from Apple. While measures quite as extreme as Jobs' may not be necessary, getting comfortable with and seeking out varied, chaotic,

---

305. "Steve Jobs on Creativity," *Farnam Street* (blog), updated November 9, 2019.
306. Walter Isaacson, *Steve Jobs*, (New York: Simon & Schuster, 2011).

and sometimes unpleasant life experiences may indeed be a hidden component to success.

One thing that doesn't count as *life experience* is living in a bubble. Going to your same grocery store every week and shopping for the same ingredients to cook into the same meals you ate last week is an example of a bubble. Any day that blends into the next is a missed opportunity for your next breakthrough on the path to exponential growth. While some semblance of regularity in your life can help you stay on track toward your goals, too much routine is a creativity killer.

One of the reasons immigrants and their children may find disproportionate success is that hardship begets resilience. Moving away from your home culture and plopping your family down in Tulsa, Brooklyn, or Palo Alto is bound to be a chaotic, stressful challenge. Those with antifragile systems will benefit from this uncertainty and use it to their advantage. With both the grit and creative inputs that come from a difficult situation, immigrants find themselves at a prime intersection for benefiting from chaos.

Just as plants are dissipative structures by turning light into usable energy, the human mind can turn chaos into strength. Courage, resilience, perseverance, and stress tolerance are all ways the mind can manage, and even benefit, from stressors. "Without [these strategies], we would be constantly suffering through the random bombardment of stray psychological meteorites," Csikszentmihalyi writes.[307]

So how do you develop these characteristics in your own life? It just so happens that there are techniques that have been used by people for centuries to address this exact question.

---

307. Csikszentmihalyi, *Flow*, 202.

Stoicism & Travel

We've all heard the old adage, "What doesn't kill you makes you stronger," but most people don't seek out difficult or straining experiences just for the fun of it. But what would happen if you did decide to go hunting for chances to test your mental grit?

Stoic philosophy is built around the concept of internal strength. One technique for building this strength is seeking out voluntary discomfort and intentionally putting the body through strain. This practice is nothing new; we do it every time we exercise. Another way to build this kind of strength is to renounce our cushy lifestyles for periods of time. The great philosopher Epictetus advised people to reduce their reliance on the creature comforts of everyday life by periodically removing them.[308] Modern day stoic thinkers encourage practices like fasting, taking cold showers, and even sleeping on the floor to build resilience and adaptability.

If you don't want to live an ascetic or stoic lifestyle, a great solution is to travel. By being a low-budget traveler, not a tourist, you expose yourself to both beautiful and difficult life situations that may change the way you view the world. In the book *Vagabonding*, author Rolf Potts describes the freedom of traveling with minimal possessions, occasionally sleeping in fields, and leaning in to the unpredictability of long-term, low-budget exploration. "You should view each new travel frustration—sickness, fear, loneliness, boredom,

---

308. Isaac Chanakira, "3 Practical and Effective Stoic Exercises from Marcus Aurelius, Seneca and Epictetus," *Daily Stoic* (blog), Daily Stoic, updated August 8, 2017.

conflict—as just another curious facet in the vagabonding adventure," he wrote.[309]

Personally, I have never been a deeper sleeper than when I spent ten months living in cheap hostels around Asia and Oceania. Within the first month, I could withstand any disturbance at night—be it loud party goers or accomplished snorers. In each unknown bed over the many weeks, I would fall asleep quickly and sink into a deep, restful place until morning.

Since returning from my travels, however, my tolerance for sleep disruption has dissipated greatly. These days, a distant car horn or small amount of light in the room will wake me up and keep me up for hours. Resilience and anti-fragility, it seems, must be constantly rebuilt and tested for maximum potency.

Low-budget travel, but also exercise, meditation, fasting or dieting, learning a new skill or language, and anything else that tests your willpower, patience, and internal fortitude helps you stay above the surface when, inevitably, a tsunami of chaos hits. Lean into it, and you might just enjoy the struggle. I've heard this described as type II fun, the kind of fun that isn't objectively enjoyable in the moment, but looking back, it was a great time.

Hunter S. Thompson said, "Life should not be a journey to the grave with the intention of arriving safely in a pretty and well-preserved body but rather to skid in broadside in a cloud of smoke, thoroughly used up, totally worn out, and loudly proclaiming 'Wow! What a ride!'"[310] We should seek

309. Rolf Potts, *Vagabonding: An Uncommon Guide to the Art of Long-Term World Travel*, (New York: Ballantine Books, 2016).

310. Hunter S. Thompson, "A Quote from The Proud Highway," *Goodreads*, Goodreads, accessed March 10, 2021.

out and relish this adventure, this struggle, for the experience it gives us and the character it builds.

Preserving Optionality

Now, chaos, of course, can be disruptive. It can destroy what has been built, leach energy from the important things, and create a world of confusion and disaster. Mitigating chaos, to some extent, is a good strategy. You wouldn't want to drive with a blindfold on, neglect to do the dishes for three months, or adopt a bunch of animals from the zoo just to see what happens.

As a fundamental law of physics, there's really no way around encountering chaos. The Second Law of Thermodynamics says that entropy always increases. Chaos leaks out any time anything happens. Even if you leave your house completely alone for a month and hightail it to Hawaii, the house will still collect dust. Every time you start your car, a little bit of the ignition energy is lost to heat. There is no process in existence where a little bit of energy isn't lost to entropy.

The upside is that chaos encourages us to keep our options open as a failsafe for disaster. The mental model for this is called preserving optionality.[311] Preserving optionality means "strategically keeping your options open." Emphasis lies on the strategic part. At some point, you have to make choices, pick a lane, and grind toward a specific goal or outcome. Defining this outcome too soon can have large consequences, but waiting too long to decide is its equal and opposite reaction.

---

311. "Preserving Optionality: Preparing for the Unknown," *Farnam Street* (blog), updated March 23, 2020.

Preserving optionality allows people and companies to adjust their behavior after gathering more information. This ties back to the Bayesian updating mental model we talked about in chapter eleven. When Google first started, it tried to make money selling search appliances to large companies.[312] It didn't work. Had they kept this as their main focus, the company probably wouldn't be what it is today. Instead, Google preserved optionality, building out its interface and data capabilities and eventually monetizing its advertising arm, AdWords.

In the startup world, settling for less than what you are worth kills optionality. Reid Hoffman, one of the PayPal Mafia members and later cofounder of LinkedIn, talks about PayPal's many exit options and their strategic moves. Before PayPal's IPO Peter Thiel sent Hoffman on a mission to sell the company for $600 million.[313] VeriSign offered $550 million, but PayPal declined and decided to keep other options on the table. After turning down the offer, the employees continued to build and grow the company, coming to believe it was worth about $1 billion. Next, eBay stepped in and offered $850 million. Once again, the employees turned down the lowball offer and instead decided to go public. In the end, eBay bought PayPal for $1.5 billion.

How do you know when to trade your optionality in for big returns? Hoffman's advice is to build strategic value.[314] The more valuable you make your product or skill, the better the offers will get. At a certain point, strategy indicates

312. Reid Hoffman, "M&A Or IPO?" *Greylock*, Greylock Partners, July 23, 2020.
313. Ibid.
314. Ibid.

that it is more advantageous to exercise your options than to keep them.

For PayPal, joining eBay reached a tipping point where it became more strategic to collaborate than to remain independent. Before the acquisition, eBay had been actively discouraging its users from using PayPal, and the friction wasn't sustainable. After the acquisition, PayPal saw enormous gains from the support of the parent company. PayPal sits comfortably in the $300 billion dollar range today.[315] Preserving optionality until a window of opportunity opened increased the company's value from its first starting point by about 50,000 percent.

In order for all of this to occur, Hoffman and other PayPal employees had to lash themselves to the mast during the storm, weather out the buffeting waves, and pray the tempest would land them safe and secure. By riding out the chaos, they found the hidden treasure that wouldn't have been available to them otherwise.

Preserving optionality in chasing your personal moonshot means you open yourself up to the many variations of how it could occur. Perhaps you'll end up achieving success in a completely different manner than you anticipated, or perhaps the moonshot itself will shift from your original vision. Terrence McKenna wrote, "The creative act is a letting down of the net of human imagination into the ocean of chaos on which we are suspended, and the attempt to bring out of it ideas."[316] Sometimes we must try and make order of the chaos, as with personal knowledge management,

---

315. "PayPal Holdings Net Worth 2013-2020: PYPL," *Macrotrends*, Macrotrends LLC, accessed February 7, 2021.

316. Terence McKenna, "A Quote by Terence McKenna," *Goodreads*, Goodreads, accessed March 10, 2021.

sometimes we must use it as a tool, like to identify loose connections, and sometimes, we must simply sink into it, allowing it to flow over us and wash away what is old and bring to us what is new.

In any case, one thing is certain: Chaos will happen. Learning to embrace it builds up your systems, your strength of mind, and your options to adapt along the way.

CONCLUSION

———

There is only one success—to be able to spend your
life in your own way.

—CHRISTOPHER MORLEY

Archimedes levers are everywhere. With the right mental
lens, you can begin to see them and strategically position
yourself to be lifted up high. Humans will continue to be
bad at estimating the effects of exponential growth, but that
makes it all the more exciting. When you catch a window
of opportunity, take it; you don't know exactly where you'll
end up. You may find yourself much further along than you
ever dreamed of being.

Moonshots are inherently nebulous and ambiguous. Do
not be dissuaded by the fear that people won't like what you
have to offer.

As we explored in chapter five, you can find a thousand
true fans doing just about anything—even selling something
you think nobody will want. In 1961, Artist Piero Manzoni
sealed his own excrement into ninety tin cans. He titled the

works "Artist's Shit" and they sold for their weight in gold.[317] Today, the pieces still find their way into auctions and continue to sell for the updated price of gold, typically for hundreds of thousands of dollars. Manzoni loved art and enjoyed success by doing something no one else was doing, no matter how off-putting. Unencumbered by fear of ridicule or failure, he made history in his own way.

Another person who loves what he does so much that he isn't afraid to attempt the impossible is eighty-three-year-old Reverend Robert Evans, the man who hunts death. Armed with a telescope and a patch of sky between gum trees, the semi-retired minister sits outside on his porch in the Blue Mountains of Australia and looks for supernovae, the explosions of dying stars.

Evans is exceptional at finding them. To date, he has spotted forty-two supernovae, the most ever recorded for visual discoveries. The only things that can rival his incredible ability are complex computer programs trained to detect infinitesimal differences in the patterns of galaxies.[318]

Noteworthy amateur astronomers are rare, but Evans has never been deterred. Using only his telescope and star charts, he has spent the past few decades sitting and watching, quietly outperforming every other trained astronomer who has ever tried to find the dying stars.

Author Bill Bryson sums up the difficulty of the task in *A Short History of Nearly Everything:*

> To understand what a feat this is, imagine a standard dining room table covered in a black tablecloth and

317. "'Artist's Shit', Piero Manzoni, 1961," Tate, accessed March 1 2021.
318. Anne Barrowclough, "The Supernova Hunter," *The Australian,* The Weekend Australian Magazine, July 21, 2018.

someone throwing a handful of salt across it. The scattered grains can be thought of as a galaxy. Now imagine fifteen hundred more tables like the first one—enough to fill a Wal-Mart parking lot, say, or to make a single line two miles long—each with a random array of salt across it. Now add one grain of salt to any table and let Bob Evans walk among them. At a glance, he will spot it. That grain of salt is the supernova.[319]

In the true character of someone simply doing what he loves, Evans is nonchalant about his achievements. "I just seem to have a knack for memorizing star fields," he told Bryson, "I'm not particularly good at other things. I don't remember names well."[320]

Evans embodies the perfect formula for success: He loves what he does, pairs it with a unique skillset, and chases a goal few dare attempt. To date, he has won numerous awards from astronomy societies around the globe and has received international praise.

Loving your pursuit is paramount. Evans didn't decide to hunt supernovae out of a desire for glory or because someone told him to. He chased his natural intuition and became infatuated enough that he kept up his search, even through a three-year period where he didn't discover a single thing. Anyone other than a true supernovae connoisseur would have thrown in the towel, thus, loving what you do is the final ingredient to the moonshot pursuit.

The beauty of so many of the concepts we explored in this book—pursuing your passion, surrounding yourself with

319. Bill Bryson, *A Short History of Nearly Everything*, (London: Black Swan, 2016) 27.
320. Ibid.

giving and driven people, getting into flow state, inducing luck, embracing chaos, loving what you do—is that they are genuinely enjoyable endeavors. Make sure to experience them. The exhilaration of riding on a moonshot rocket comes when you stick your head up and look around. The goal is to chase your moonshot with everything you've got and to appreciate every minute of it. After all, success isn't an end state; it's a moving target. Whatever is worth chasing for eternity is worth enjoying.

In the end, meaning is what triumphs. "If you have some success early in life, you get to find out early it doesn't mean anything," David Foster Wallace said, "which means you get to start early the work of figuring out what does mean something."[321] Success alone won't fulfil you. Chasing a moonshot, then, is about finding what matters the most to you in life, brings you joy, uses your talents to their fullest abilities, allows you to cross paths with the most energizing, interesting people who believe in what you want to achieve, and growing your dream so massive that it invites the whole world to feel what you feel.

Toni Morrison reminds us to bring others along on our journey. "I tell my students, 'When you get these jobs that you have been so brilliantly trained for, just remember that your real job is that if you are free, you need to free somebody else. If you have some power, then your job is to empower somebody else.'"[322]

---

321. David Lipsky, *Although of Course You End up Becoming Yourself: A Road Trip with David Foster Wallace*, Google Books. (New York: Broadway Books, 2010) 69.

322. Pam Houston, "The Truest Eye," Oprah.com, Harpo, Inc., updated November 2003.

The Apollo 11 astronauts took millions of viewers along with them on their own moonshot journey. When Neil Armstrong and Buzz Aldrin took their fortuitus first steps on the moon, the 650 million people watching on their television sets at home got a collective chill down their spines.[323] The victory was shared. In the end, after exponential success sinks in, the goal is to step on the other side of that lever and elevate the rest of the world.

This is the art of the moonshot.

---

323. Sarah Loff, "Apollo 11 Mission Overview," *NASA*, NASA, updated May 15, 2019.

ACKNOWLEDGMENTS

It took an incredible launch team to help me reach this moonshot. Thank you to everyone who did their best at keeping me sane during this process. It partially worked.

Thank you to my wonderful parents for their loving support and for reading early, poorly written drafts. Thank you for living inspiring lives that encourage me to shoot for the moon.

Thank you to my marketing and revisions editor, Jessica Fleischman, for your warm encouragement and excellent edits, and to Eric Koester who paved the way for thousands of authors to benefit from a wonderful writing program, myself included.

Thank you to Alex, who supported me every step of the way and through the steepest of deadlines, and to Warren and Sue, who let me use their home as a writer's refuge. To Sumner, Lizzie, Rose, Cass, and Maddy for being my people since the days when I had a bowl cut; thank you for always making me smile on the phone and in person. To Cam, who inspires me every day by chasing his own moonshot. To Eliza and Dani and Cait, who made the dark winter nights warm and bright. Thank you to Jon, for his unending belief in me. To Jack, who pursues what he loves every day. To Kevin, Chase, Zach, Tavin, Sam, Chris, Eva, and Isis for the wonderful phone calls of support. To Molly King and Aunt Brenda, who championed my ideas online. And to the Gills, for being my second family and even bringing me turkey on Thanksgiving.

This book was only possible due to the support of people who believed in me before ever seeing a piece of my writing. Thank you to:

Robert Bojs, Madi Sellers, Tim Hanlon, Caroline Montague, Ethan Turer, Casey Lutz, Will Strand, Jacob Arlington, Andie Creel, Christine Coughlin, Kyle and Drew Rozean, John Collins, Kris Thomas, Kalen Goo and the Cal Poly Entrepreneurs, Anne Goertzen, Hale Tussing, Emily Cain, Ariel Riggan, Kaitlyn Todd, John Waidhofer, Maggie Weiss, Melly Reuling, Optimotive.co, Deidre Combs, Ed Dratz, Ben Tweedy, Emma Reynolds, Samantha Gilbert, Stacey Tompkins, Dylan Reynolds, The McChesneys, Dick Dorworth, Lori Lawson, Isaac Nelson, Billie Warford, Linda Young, Emily Richardson, Rob Hutchison, Tambra Zimmermann, Pierre Vacheresse, Alex (Bill) Yee, Eli Rosenthal, Maysa Cepra Crooks, Alexa Rozell, Claire Lewinski, Will Ward, Talia Worth, Alex Govig, Mitch Schafhauser, Olive Fontaine, Sophie Hosbein, and Stoyan Shukerov.

APPENDIX

Introduction

Fitzgerald, F. Scott. *The Great Gatsby*. New York: Scribner Paperback Fiction, 1995.

"Personal Development Market Size Worth $56.66 Billion by 2027." Grand View Research Inc. July 27, 2020. https://www.prnewswire.com/news-releases/personal-development-market-size-worth-56-66-billion-by-2027-grand-view-research-inc-301099976.html.

Wallace, David Foster. *Infinite Jest*. Boston: Little, Brown and Company, 1996. https://books.google.com/books?id=Nhe2yvx6hP8C&vq=claw+marks&source=gbs_navlinks_s.

Chapter 1: Levers & Leverage

"Archimedes Death Ray." Ignite. Massachusetts Institute of Technology, updated October 2005. http://web.mit.edu/2.009/www/experiments/deathray/10_ArchimedesResult.html.

Banayan, Alex. *The Third Door: The Wild Quest to Uncover How the World's Most Successful People Launched Their Careers.* New York: Currency, 2018, inside cover.

"Career Change Report: An Inside Look at Why Workers Shift Gears." Lead. Indeed, October 30, 2019. https://www.indeed.com/lead/career-change.

Morgan, Morris Hickey. *Vitruvius: The Ten Books on Architecture.* Cambridge: Harvard University Press, 1914, quoted in "The Ten Books on Architecture." The Golden Crown. Accessed February 2, 2021. https://www.math.nyu.edu/~crorres/Archimedes/Crown/Vitruvius.html.

New World Encyclopedia. s.v. "Lever." Accessed March 8, 2021. https://www.newworldencyclopedia.org/entry/Lever.

O'Connor, J. J., and E. F. Robertson. "Archimedes—Biography." Maths History. *School of Mathematics and Statistics University of St Andrews,* January 1999. https://mathshistory.st-andrews.ac.uk/Biographies/Archimedes/.

Philps, Rhiannon. "The Ultimate Guide to the FIRE Movement." *NerdWallet.* NerdWallet Ltd. Accessed January 20, 2021. https://www.nerdwallet.com/uk/current-accounts/guide-to-the-fire-movement/.

Pollard, Justin, and Howard Reid. *The Rise and Fall of Alexandria: Birthplace of the Modern Mind. Google Books.* New York: Viking, 2006. https://books.google.com/books?id=Y5bg1LOJJXoC.

Roche, Julia La. "Here's How Much 10 of The Richest People in the World Made per Minute in 2013." *Business Insider.* Business Insider. Updated December 19, 2013. https://www.businessinsider.com/what-warren-buffett-makes-per-hour-2013-12.

Rorres, Chris. "The Lever Quotations." Archimedes. Accessed January 20, 2021. https://www.math.nyu.edu/~crorres/Archimedes/Lever/LeverQuotes.html.

Ross, Rachel. "Eureka! The Archimedes Principle." LiveScience. Future US. Updated April 26, 2017. https://www.livescience.com/58839-archimedes-principle.html.

Salata, Mark. "How Taking a Bath Led to Archimedes' Principle." TED. TED-Ed. Accessed February 26, 2021. https://ed.ted.com/lessons/mark-salata-how-taking-a-bath-led-to-archimedes-principle.

Steincamp, Isaac. "The Youngest Chess Grandmasters in History." Chess.com. Updated February 27, 2020. https://www.chess.com/article/view/youngest-chess-grandmasters.

"What Is Buoyant Force?" *Khan Academy*. Khan Academy. Accessed February 26, 2021. https://www.khanacademy.org/science/physics/fluids/buoyant-force-and-archimedes-principle/a/buoyant-force-and-archimedes-principle-article.

Chapter 2: Understanding the Exponential

"13 Common Items That Weigh about 30 Pounds." Weight of Stuff. Weight of Stuff, August 23, 2020. https://weightofstuff.com/13-common-items-that-weigh-about-30-pounds/.

Bonchek, Mark. "How to Create an Exponential Mindset." *Harvard Business Review*. Harvard Business Review, October 4, 2017. https://hbr.org/2016/07/how-to-create-an-exponential-mindset.

"Calories in 1 Cup of Ice Cream and Nutrition Facts." *FatSecret*. FatSecret. Accessed March 5, 2021. https://www.fatsecret.com/calories-nutrition/generic/ice-cream?portionid=1772&portionamount=1.000.

Diamandis, Peter H., and Steven Kotler. *The Future Is Faster than You Think: How Converging Technologies Are Transforming Business, Industries, and Our Lives*. New York: Simon & Schuster, 2020.

Frohlich, Thomas C, and John Harrington. "The Heaviest Objects in the World." *MSN News*. Microsoft News. Updated May 11, 2018. https://www.msn.com/en-us/news/money/the-heaviest-objects-in-the-world/ar-AAx8KwU.

Gabriel, Kaigham J. "How to Fight 'Eroom's Law.'" *Scientific American Blog Network*. Scientific American, July 9, 2019. https://blogs.scientificamerican.com/observations/how-to-fight-erooms-law/.

Gladwell, Malcolm. *The Tipping Point: How Little Things Can Make a Big Difference*. Boston: Back Bay Books / Little, Brown and Company, 2002.

Khallikan, Ibn. *Ibn Khallikan's Biographical Dictionary*. Translated by William MacGuckin Slane. *Google Books* 3. Vol. 3, 1970. https://books.google.com.tr/books?id=-8dLAAAAcAAJ.

Kurzweil, Ray. "The Law of Accelerating Returns." *Kurzweil Accelerating Intelligence*. Kurzweil Network, March 7, 2001. https://www.kurzweilai.net/the-law-of-accelerating-returns.

Levy, Matthew R., and Joshua Tasoff. "Exponential-Growth Bias and Overconfidence." *Journal of Economic Psychology* 58 (February 2017): 1-14. https://doi.org/10.1016/j.joep.2016.11.001.

Encyclopedia Britannica. s.v. "Moore's Law." Accessed February 16, 2021. https://www.britannica.com/technology/Moores-law.

Nova, Annie. "10 Unlikely Products That Made Millions of Dollars." *CNBC*. CNBC, December 11, 2017. https://www.cnbc.com/2017/12/11/10-unlikely-products-that-made-millions-of-dollars.html.

Paenza, Adrian. "How Folding Paper Can Get You to the Moon." TED. TED-Ed. Accessed February 17, 2021. https://ed.ted.com/lessons/how-folding-paper-can-get-you-to-the-moon.

Shellenberger, Michael. "If Solar Panels Are So Clean, Why Do They Produce So Much Toxic Waste?" *Forbes*. Forbes, updated May 28, 2019. https://www.forbes.com/sites/

michaelshellenberger/2018/05/23/if-solar-panels-are-so-clean-why-do-they-produce-so-much-toxic-waste/?sh=dec1ca1121cc.

Shoukat, Sehar. "Cell Phone Addiction and Psychological and Physiological Health in Adolescents." *EXCLI Journal* 18 (February 4, 2019): 47-50. https://www.ncbi.nlm.nih.gov/pmc/articles/PMC6449671/.

"Solar Explained." Solar Energy and the Environment. U.S. Energy Information Administration, September 23, 2020. https://www.eia.gov/energyexplained/solar/solar-energy-and-the-environment.php.

Tardi, Carla. "Moore's Law Explained." *Investopedia*. Investopedia, September 16, 2020. https://www.investopedia.com/terms/m/mooreslaw.asp.

Thiel, Peter. *Zero to One: Notes on Startups, or How to Build the Future*. London: Virgin Books, 2014.

Zax, David. "Is Your Cell Phone Helping to Fund a Civil War?" Smithsonian.com. Smithsonian Institution, October 1, 2013. https://www.smithsonianmag.com/innovation/is-your-cell-phone-helping-to-fund-a-civil-war-7654/.

Chapter 3: Direction & Magnitude

Altman, Sam. "The Strength of Being Misunderstood." *Sam Altman* (blog). Sam Altman, Accessed February 26, 2020. https://blog.samaltman.com/hard-startups.

Altman, Sam (@sama). "The expected value of your impact on the world is like a vector." Twitter. August 24, 2020. https://twitter.com/sama/status/1297912739206242306.

Blacklock, Amy. "How to Achieve an Exponential Mindset." Wealthfit, Accessed January 7, 2021. https://wealthfit.com/articles/exponential-thinking-mindset/.

Collins, Jim, and Jerry I. Porras. "BHAG—Big Hairy Audacious Goal." *Jim Collins* (blog). Jim Collins, Accessed January 13, 2021. https://www.jimcollins.com/article_topics/articles/BHAG.html.

Eliason, Nat. "Forget Commitment: Invest in Something." *Nat Eliason* (blog). December 1, 2020. https://www.nateliason.com/blog/invest-in-something.

Gawdat, Mo. "How One Google Engineer Turned Tragedy into a Moonshot." Other. HBR IdeaCast. *Harvard Business Review*, January 2, 2019. https://hbr.org/podcast/2019/01/how-one-google-engineer-turned-tragedy-into-a-moonshot.

Gawdat, Mo. "The Mission." A Billion People Happy. Onebillionhappy. Updated June 18, 2019. https://www.onebillionhappy.org/about/.

"How Fast Should You Be Growing?" *TechCrunch*. TechCrunch. August 24, 2013. https://techcrunch.com/2013/08/24/how-fast-should-you-be-growing/.

Jain, Naveen, and John Schroeter. *Moonshots: Creating a World of Abundance*. New York: Moonshots Press, 2018.

Mitsuhashi, Yukari. "Ikigai: A Japanese Concept to Improve Work and Life." *BBC Worklife*. BBC, August 7, 2017. https://www.bbc.com/worklife/article/20170807-ikigai-a-japanese-concept-to-improve-work-and-life.

"One Third of Your Life Is Spent at Work." *News*. Gettysburg College. Accessed January 11, 2021. https://www.gettysburg.edu/news/stories?id=79db7b34-630c-4f49-ad32-4ab9ea48e72b.

"Projects." X, the Moonshot Factory. X Development LLC. Accessed March 5, 2021. https://x.company/projects/.

Schippers, Michaéla C., and Niklas Ziegler. "Life Crafting as a Way to Find Purpose and Meaning in Life." *Frontiers in Psychology* 10, no. 2778. Accessed January 12, 2021. https://doi.org/10.3389/fpsyg.2019.02778.

Simon, Herbert A. "Rational Choice and the Structure of the Environment." *Psychological Review* 2 (1956): 129-38. https://psycnet.apa.org/record/1957-01985-001.

Tucker, Ian. "Google's Mo Gawdat: 'Happiness Is Like Keeping Fit. You Have to Work Out'." *The Guardian*. Guardian News and Media, April 30, 2017. https://www.theguardian.com/technology/2017/apr/30/google-mo-gawdat-solve-for-happy-interview.

Waude, Adam. "Maximizers vs. Satisficers: Who Makes Better Decisions?" *Psychologist World*, December 14, 2016. https://www.psychologistworld.com/cognitive/maximizers-satisficers-decision-making.

"Text of Steve Jobs' Commencement Address (2005)." *Stanford News.* Stanford University, June 12, 2017. https://news.stanford.edu/2005/06/14/jobs-061505/.

Yang, Mu-Li, and Wen-Bin Chiou. "Looking Online for the Best Romantic Partner Reduces Decision Quality: The Moderating Role of Choice-Making Strategies." *CyberPsychology & Behavior* 13 (April 2009). https://doi.org/10.1089/cpb.2009.0208.

Chapter 4: The Toolkit

Buehlman, Kim T., John M. Gottman, and Lynn F. Katz. "How a Couple Views Their Past Predicts Their Future: Predicting Divorce from an Oral History Interview." *Journal of Family Psychology* 5, no. 3-4 (1992): 295-318. https://doi.org/10.1037/0893-3200.5.3-4.295.

Clear, James. *Atomic Habits: An Easy & Proven Way to Build Good Habits & Break Bad Ones.* New York: Random House, 2018.

Cunff, Anne-Laure Le. "Building Intrinsic Motivation." *Ness Labs.* Ness Labs, May 5, 2020. https://nesslabs.com/intrinsic-motivation-3.

Cunff, Anne-Laure Le. "SMART Goals Are Not So Smart: Make a PACT Instead." *Ness Labs*. Ness Labs, July 13, 2020. https://nesslabs.com/smart-goals-pact.

Dyson, James. "No Innovator's Dilemma Here: In Praise of Failure." *Wired*. Conde Nast, September 11, 2018. https://www.wired.com/2011/04/in-praise-of-failure/.

"Engineering the Future." The James Dyson Foundation. The James Dyson Foundation North America. Accessed March 6, 2021. https://www.jamesdysonfoundation.com/.

"Goal Setting." MIT Human Resources. Massachusetts Institute of Technology. Accessed February 3, 2021. https://hr.mit.edu/performance/goals.

Harari, Yuval Noah. "Yuval Noah Harari Extract: 'Humans Have Always Lived in the Age of Post-Truth. We're a Post-Truth Species.'" *The Guardian*. Guardian News and Media, August 5, 2018. https://www.theguardian.com/culture/2018/aug/05/yuval-noah-harari-extract-fake-news-sapiens-homo-deus.

"Hasan Minhaj Didn't Become a Lawyer." *NPR*. NPR, November 14, 2018. https://www.npr.org/2018/11/14/667842189/hasan-minhaj-didnt-become-a-lawyer.

Herman, Todd. *The Alter Ego Effect: The Power of Secret Identities to Transform Your Life*, 2. New York: Harper Collins Publishers, 2019.

Horowitz, Ben. "What You Do Is Who You Are." Andreessen Horowitz. Accessed February 10, 2021. https://a16z.com/book/whatyoudo/.

Iyengar, Sheena S, and Mark R Lepper. "When Choice Is Demotivating: Can One Desire Too Much of a Good Thing." *Journal of Personality and Social Psychology*, (January 2001), 995-1006. https://doi.org/10.1037/0022-3514.79.6.995.

Noah, Trevor. "Hasan Minhaj." Pioneers. *TIME*. Accessed February 10, 2021. https://time.com/collection/100-most-influential-people-2019/5567704/hasan-minhaj/.

Schwartz, Barry. "More Isn't Always Better." *Harvard Business Review.* Harvard Business Publishing, August 1, 2014. https://hbr.org/2006/06/more-isnt-always-better.

Robson, David. "The 'Batman Effect': How Having an Alter Ego Empowers You." *The Life Project.* BBC, August 17, 2020. https://www.bbc.com/worklife/article/20200817-the-batman-effect-how-having-an-alter-ego-empowers-you.

Talks at Google, "Grit: The Power of Passion and Perseverance | Angela Duckworth | Talks at Google." May 6, 2016. Video, 51:59. https://youtu.be/W-ONEAcBeTk.

Timar, Brian. "Mimetic Traps." *Brian Timar* (blog), May 19, 2019. https://www.briantimar.com/notes/mimetic/mimetic/.

Touré. "Adele Opens Up About Her Inspirations, Looks, and Stage Fright." *Rolling Stone.* Rolling Stone, June 25, 2018. https://www.rollingstone.com/music/music-news/adele-opens-up-about-her-inspirations-looks-and-stage-fright-79626/.

Chapter 5: Big Fish, Small Pond

Awan, Aatif. "The Power of LinkedIn's 500 Million Member Community." *LinkedIn Official Blog.* LinkedIn Corporation, April 24, 2017. https://blog.linkedin.com/2017/april/24/the-power-of-linkedins-500-million-community.

Blank, Steve. "Why the Lean Start-Up Changes Everything." *Entrepreneurship. Harvard Business Review.* February 9, 2018. https://hbr.org/2013/05/why-the-lean-start-up-changes-everything.

Brown, Meta S. "Why Nate Silver's Forecasts Are Better Than Yours (And How You Can Improve)." *Forbes.* Forbes Magazine, July 31, 2016. https://www.forbes.com/sites/metabrown/2016/07/31/

why-nate-silvers-forecasts-are-better-than-yours-and-how-to-improve-yours/?sh=3f3a0e4b7bcf.

Cerullo, Megan. "Influencer Marketing Fraud Will Cost Brands $1.3 Billion in 2019." *CBS News*. CBS Interactive, July 25, 2019. https://www.cbsnews.com/news/influencer-marketing-fraud-costs-companies-1-3-billion/.

Crawford, Krysten. "Stanford Education Study Provides New Evidence of 'Big-Fish-Little-Pond' Effect on Students Globally." *Research Stories*. Stanford University, December 13, 2018. https://ed.stanford.edu/news/stanford-education-study-provides-new-evidence-big-fish-little-pond-effect-students-globally.

Dubner, Stephen J. "FREAK-Quently Asked Questions: Nate Silver." *Freakonomics*. Freakonomics, LLC, March 12, 2009. https://freakonomics.com/2009/03/12/freak-quently-asked-questions-nate-silver/.

"Fivethirtyeight.com Traffic Statistics." *SimilarWeb*. SimilarWeb LTD. Accessed January 19, 2021. https://www.similarweb.com/website/fivethirtyeight.com/#overview.

Godin, Seth. "1000 True Fans." *Seth's Blog*. March 4, 2008. https://seths.blog/2008/03/1000-true-fans/.

Hartmans, Avery. "'Amazon' Wasn't the Original Name of Jeff Bezos' Company, and 14 Other Little-Known Facts about the Early Days of Amazon." *Business Insider*. Business Insider. February 3, 2021. https://www.businessinsider.com/jeff-bezos-amazon-history-facts-2017-4.

Kelly, Kevin. "1,000 True Fans." *The Technium* (blog), March 4, 2008. https://kk.org/thetechnium/1000-true-fans/.

Kordestani, Milan. "Building in Public: How Tech Companies Master Product-Market Fit." *Entrepreneur*. Entrepreneur Media, November 13, 2020. https://www.entrepreneur.com/article/359180.

"r/BreadStapledToTrees." reddit. Accessed February 17, 2021.

https://www.reddit.com/r/BreadStapledToTrees/.

Romano, Andrew. "Polling: Baseball's Stat Star on Campaign '08." *Newsweek*. Newsweek, June 7, 2008. https://www.newsweek.com/polling-baseballs-stat-star-campaign-08-90937.

Saint, Nick. "If You're Not Embarrassed by the First Version of Your Product, You've Launched Too Late." *Business Insider*. Business Insider, November 13, 2009. https://www.businessinsider.com/the-iterate-fast-and-release-often-philosophy-of-entrepreneurship-2009-11.

Silver, Nate. "El Taco Veloz [#2] Defeats Picante Taqueria [#10]." *The Burrito Bracket* (blog), November 10, 2007. https://burritobracket.blogspot.com/.

Silver, Nate. "In Search of America's Best Burrito." *FiveThirtyEight*. FiveThirtyEight, June 5, 2014. https://fivethirtyeight.com/features/in-search-of-americas-best-burrito/.

Sternbergh, Adam. "How Nate Silver Went from Forecasting Baseball Games to Forecasting Elections." *New York Magazine*. New York Magazine, October 9, 2008. https://nymag.com/news/features/51170/.

Thiel, Peter. *Zero to One: Notes on Startups, or How to Build the Future*. London: Virgin Books, 2014.

Turck, Matt (@mattturck). Twitter. February 22, 2021. https://twitter.com/mattturck/status/1363960322537771015.

Chapter 6: The Pareto Principle

Best, Mark and Duncan Neuhauser. "Joseph Juran: Overcoming Resistance to Organizational Change." *Quality and Safety in Health Care*, no. 5 (2006): 380-82.

Coelho, Paulo and Alan Clarke. *The Alchemist*. New York: Harper-One, 2018.

Davis, Nicola. "High Social Cost Adults Can Be Predicted from as Young as Three, Says Study." *The Guardian*. December 12, 2016. https://www.theguardian.com/science/2016/dec/12/high-social-cost-adults-can-be-identified-from-as-young-as-three-says-study.

Hall, Mary. "Real-Life Examples of the 80-20 Rule (Pareto Principle) in Practice." *Investopedia*. Investopedia, November 6, 2020. https://www.investopedia.com/ask/answers/050115/what-are-some-reallife-examples-8020-rule-pareto-principle-practice.asp.

N. R. Kleinfield, "A Tight Squeeze at Video Stores," *The New York Times*, May 1, 1988. https://www.nytimes.com/1988/05/01/business/a-tight-squeeze-at-video-stores.html.

Koch, Richard. *The 80/20 Principle: The Secret of Achieving More with Less*. 3.1. Vol. 3.1. New York: Doubleday, 2008.

Newman, M. E. J. "Power Laws, Pareto Distributions and Zipf's Law." Department of Physics and Center for the Study of Complex Systems University of Michigan, Ann Arbor, May 29, 2006. https://arxiv.org/PS_cache/cond-mat/pdf/0412/0412004v3.pdf.

Rispoli, Fred J., Suhua Zeng, Tim Green, Jennifer Higbie. "Even Birds Follow Pareto's 80-20 Rule." *Significance* 11, no. 1 (February 2014): 37-38.

Sivers, Derek. "Hell Yeah or No: What's Worth Doing." *Derek Sivers* (blog). Accessed March 6, 2021. https://sive.rs/n.

Chapter 7: In Flow

"About Steven Kotler: High Performance Expert." Steven Kotler: Author and Speaker. Accessed February 13, 2021. https://www.stevenkotler.com/about.

Barton, Laura. "Cabin Fever." *The Guardian*. Guardian News & Media Limited, May 14, 2008. https://www.theguardian.com/ music/2008/may/14/popandrock.boniver.

Cain, Susan. *Quiet: The Power of Introverts in a World That Can't Stop Talking*. New York: Broadway Paperbacks, 2013.

Cranston, Susie, and Scott Keller. "Increasing the 'Meaning Quotient' of Work." *McKinsey & Company*. McKinsey & Company, January 1, 2013. https://www.mckinsey.com/business-functions/organization/our-insights/increasing-the-meaning-quotient-of-work.

Csikszentmihalyi, Mihaly. "Flow, the Secret to Happiness." TED. TED Conferences, February 2004. https://www.ted.com/talks/ mihaly_csikszentmihalyi_flow_the_secret_to_happiness.

de Manzano, Örjan, T. Theorell, L. Harmat, and F. Ullén. "The Psychophysiology of Flow during Piano Playing." *Emotion* 10, no. 3 (June 2010): 301-11. https://doi.org/10.1037/a0018432.

Erstling, Troy. "What Are Flow Triggers? And How Do They Work?" *The Flow Research Collective*. Flow Research Collective, July 29, 2020. https://www.flowresearchcollective.com/blog/ what-are-flow-triggers.

Holiday, Ryan. "The Guilty, Crazy Secret That Helps Me Write." *RyanHoliday.net* (blog). Ryan Holiday, April 14, 2014. https://ryanholiday.net/the-guilty-crazy-secret-that-helps-me-write/.

Kasa, Mark, and Zaiton Hassan. "Antecedent and Consequences of Flow: Lessons for Developing Human Resources." *Procedia— Social and Behavioral Sciences* 97 (2013): 209-13. https://doi.org/10.1016/j.sbspro.2013.10.224.

Kotler, Steven, Interview with Joe Rogan. "#873 Steven Kotler." The Joe Rogan Experience. *Spotify*. November 17, 2016.

Newport, Cal. *Deep Work*. New York: Grand Central Publishing, 2016.

"Steve Wozniak." Dancing with the Stars Wiki. Fandom TV. Accessed February 13, 2021. https://dancingwiththestars.fandom.com/wiki/Steve_Wozniak.

"Swearing Can Actually Increase Pain Tolerance." *ScienceDaily*. ScienceDaily, July 13, 2009. https://www.sciencedaily.com/releases/2009/07/090713085453.htm.

Chapter 8: The Whispers of Cities

Burns, Stephanie. "7 Reasons to Join a Mastermind Group." *Forbes*. Forbes Magazine, October 21, 2013. https://www.forbes.com/sites/chicceo/2013/10/21/7-reasons-to-join-a-mastermind-group/?sh=6c35a45c5deb.

Cain, Susan. *Quiet: The Power of Introverts in a World That Can't Stop Talking*. New York: Random House, 2012.

Eells, Josh. "The Solitary Fame of Bon Iver's Justin Vernon." *Rolling Stone*. Rolling Stone, June 25, 2018. https://www.rollingstone.com/music/music-news/the-solitary-fame-of-bon-ivers-justin-vernon-64307/.

Graham, Paul. "Cities and Ambition." *Paul Graham* (blog), May 2008. http://www.paulgraham.com/cities.html.

Hardesty, Larry. "Why Innovation Thrives in Cities." *MIT News*. Massachusetts Institute of Technology, June 4, 2013. https://news.mit.edu/2013/why-innovation-thrives-in-cities-0604.

Helft, Miguel. "It Pays to Have Pals in Silicon Valley." *The New York Times*. October 17, 2006. https://www.nytimes.com/2006/10/17/technology/17paypal.html.

Johnson, Steven. *Where Good Ideas Come From: The Natural History of Innovation*. New York: Riverhead Books, 2011.

McArdle, Megan. "The Message of Cities." *The Atlantic*. Atlantic Media Company, July 18, 2008. https://www.theatlantic.com/ business/archive/2008/05/the-message-of-cities/3542/.

Perell, David. "The Fruits of Friendship." *David Perell* (blog), January 19, 2021. https://perell.com/essay/fruits-of-friendship/.

"Regression Toward the Mean: An Introduction with Examples." Web log. *Farnam Street* (blog). Farnam Street Media Inc. Accessed January 18, 2021. https://fs.blog/2015/07/regression-to-the-mean/.

Robinson, Melia. "Tim Ferriss: 'You Are the Average of the Five People You Most Associate With'." *Business Insider*. Business Insider, January 11, 2017. https://www.businessinsider.com/tim-ferriss-average-of-five-people-2017-1.

"Synchronization of Metronomes." Harvard Natural Sciences Lecture Demonstrations. The President and Fellows of Harvard College. Accessed February 17, 2021. https://sciencedemonstrations.fas.harvard.edu/presentations/ synchronization-metronomes.

Thiel, Peter. *Zero to One: Notes on Startups, or How to Build the Future*. London: Virgin Books, 2014.

Pan, Wei, Gourab Ghoshal, Coco Krumme, Manuel Cebrian, and Alex Pentland. "Urban Characteristics Attributable to Density-Driven Tie Formation." *Nature Communications* 4, no. 1 (2013). https://doi.org/10.1038/ncomms2961.

Chapter 9: Give & Take

"3M's '100-Patent Woman' Audrey Sherman Explains How She Did It." 3M News Center. 3M Company, January 14, 2019. https://news.3m.com/English/3m-stories/3m-details/2019/3Ms-100-Patent-Woman-Audrey-Sherman-Explains-How-She-

Did-It/default.aspx.

Axelrod, Robert. *The Evolution of Cooperation. Stanford Engineering.* New York: Basic Books, 1984.

Barker, Eric. *Barking up the Wrong Tree: The Surprising Science Behind Why Everything You Know about Success Is (Mostly) Wrong.* New York: HarperOne, an imprint of HarperCollins Publishers, 2019.

Bidwell, Lauren. "Why Mentors Matter: A Summary of 30 Years of Research." *SAP.* SAP. Accessed January 26, 2021. https://www.sap.com/insights/hr/why-mentors-matter.html.

Feloni, Richard. "How Jimmy Fallon Made It to 'The Tonight Show' Through Exceptional Networking." *Business Insider.* Business Insider, November 6, 2014. https://www.businessinsider.com/jimmy-fallon-networking-key-to-success-2014-11.

Ferriss, Tim. "The Tim Ferriss Show Transcripts: Esther Perel (#241)." *The Tim Ferriss Show* (blog). Tim Ferriss. Updated June 1, 2018. https://tim.blog/2018/06/01/the-tim-ferriss-show-transcripts-esther-perel/.

Goldman, Andrew. "Jimmy Fallon's 7 Rules for Success." *Men's Journal.* A360 Media. Accessed January 25, 2021. https://www.mensjournal.com/features/jimmy-fallons-rules-for-success-20141016/.

Grant, Adam. "Are You a Giver or a Taker?" TED. TED Conferences. November 2016. https://www.ted.com/talks/adam_grant_are_you_a_giver_or_a_taker.

"History Timeline: Post-it® Notes." Post-it Brand. 3M. Accessed January 26, 2021. https://www.post-it.com/3M/en_US/post-it/contact-us/about-us/.

Holiday, Ryan. "23 Things I Learned about Writing, Strategy And Life from Tim Ferriss." *Medium.* Mission.org, October 19, 2018. https://medium.com/the-mission/23-things-i-learned-about-writing-strategy-and-life-from-tim-ferriss-b40bdfa892de.

Kerr, Mandi. "Jimmy Fallon's Impression of Adam Sandler Got Him Cast on 'Saturday Night Live.'" Showbiz Cheat Sheet, May 26, 2020. https://www.cheatsheet.com/entertainment/jimmy-fallon-impression-got-him-cast-on-saturday-night-live.html/.

Lebowitz, Shana, and Debanjali Bose. "Inside the Almost 30-Year Friendship of Bill Gates and Warren Buffett, Who Didn't Even Want to Meet and Now Have Each Other on Speed Dial." *Business Insider*. Business Insider, September 3, 2020. https://www.businessinsider.com/bill-gates-warren-buffett-friendship-2018-3.

Levy, Ariel. "Not Jerry Seinfeld." *New York Magazine*. New York Magazine, October 18, 1999. https://nymag.com/nymetro/arts/features/2139/.

Lynn Skittle. "This Is Water—Full version—David Foster Wallace Commencement Speech." Updated May 29, 2013. Video, 22:43. https://youtu.be/8CrOL-ydFMI.

Marshall, Sebastian, and Kai Zau. *Gateless*. Sebastian Marshall and Kai Zau. 2014.

Ravikant, Naval. "Compounding Relationships Make Life Easier." *Naval* (blog). Updated December 29, 2019. https://nav.al/relationships.

Potters, Charles, ed. "Prisoner's Dilemma." *Investopedia*. Investopedia, January 1, 2021. https://www.investopedia.com/terms/p/prisoners-dilemma.asp.

Slayback, Zak. "How to Write Update Emails That Help, Not Annoy." *Zak Slayback* (blog). Accessed January 25, 2021. https://zakslayback.com/how-to-write-update-emails-that-help-not-annoy/.

Stanford Encyclopedia of Philosophy. s.v. "Prisoner's Dilemma." By Steven Kuhn. Updated April 2, 2019. https://plato.stanford.edu/entries/prisoner-dilemma/#AxelTitForTat.

Willink, Jocko, and Leif Babin. *Extreme Ownership: How U.S. Navy SEALs Lead and Win.* New York: St. Martin's Press, 2017.

Chapter 10: The Brain Outside Your Brain

Ancient History Encyclopedia. s.v. "Petrarch." By Mark Cartwright, Updated October 22, 2020. https://www.ancient.eu/Petrarch/.

Ancient History Encyclopedia. s.v. "Plutarch." By Mark Cartwright, Updated February 25, 2016. https://www.ancient.eu/plutarch/.

Basbanes, Nicholas A. *Every Book Its Reader: The Power of the Written Word to Stir the World.* New York: Perennial, 2007.

Bohn, Roger, and James Short. "Measuring Consumer Information." *International Journal of Communication* 6 (2012): 980-1000.

Bush, Vannevar. "As We May Think." *The Atlantic.* The Atlantic, July 1945. https://www.theatlantic.com/magazine/archive/1945/07/as-we-may-think/303881/.

Eckermann, Johann Peter. *Conversations with Goethe.* New York, NY: Ungar, 1946.

Darnton, Robert. "Extraordinary Commonplaces." *The New York Review of Books.* NYREV, Inc, December 21, 2000. https://www.nybooks.com/articles/2000/12/21/extraordinary-commonplaces/.

Graham, Paul. "The Bus Ticket Theory of Genius." Paul Graham, November 2019. http://www.paulgraham.com/genius.html.

GQ. "Kendrick Lamar Meets Rick Rubin and They Have an Epic Conversation." October 20, 2016. Video, 49:47. https://youtu.be/4lPD5PtqMiE.

Holiday, Ryan. "How and Why to Keep a 'Commonplace Book.'" *Ryan Holiday* (blog), August 28, 2013. https://ryanholiday.net/how-and-why-to-keep-a-commonplace-book/.

James, William. "Great Men, Great Thoughts, and the Environment." *Atlantic Monthly*, October 1880. https://www.uky.edu/~eushe2/Pajares/jgreatmen.html.

"John Locke's Method for Common-Place Books (1685)." *The Public Domain Review*. Accessed February 1, 2021. https://publicdomainreview.org/collection/john-lockes-method-for-common-place-books-1685.

Johnson, Steven. *Where Good Ideas Come From: The Natural History of Innovation*. New York: Riverhead Books, 2011.

Kirby Ferguson. "Everything Is a Remix Remastered (2015 HD)." May 16, 2016. Video, 37:30. https://youtu.be/nJPERZDfyWc.

McLuhan, Marshall, and Lewis H. Lapham. *Understanding Media: The Extensions of Man*. Berkeley, CA: Gingko Press, 2015.

Oppezzo, Marily, and Daniel L. Schwartz. "Give Your Ideas Some Legs: The Positive Effect of Walking on Creative Thinking." *Journal of Experimental Psychology: Learning, Memory, and Cognition* 40, no. 4 (2014): 1142-52. https://doi.org/10.1037/a0036577.

Perell, David. "How to Cure Writer's Block." *David Perell*. David Perell. Accessed February 28, 2021. https://perell.com/essay/how-to-cure-writers-block/.

Pfuntner, Deborah Lynn. "Romantic Women Writers and Their Commonplace Books." *OakTrust*. Texas A&M University Libraries, 2016. https://oaktrust.library.tamu.edu/handle/1969.1/158136.

Schenkman, Lauren. "In the Brain, Seven Is a Magic Number." *Phys.org*. Phys.org, November 23, 2009. https://phys.org/news/2009-11-brain-magic.html.

Seidl, David, and Hannah Mormann. "Niklas Luhmann as Organization Theorist." *Oxford Handbook of Sociology, Social Theory and Organization Studies*, January 2015, 125-57. https://www.researchgate.net/publication/278131440_Niklas_Luhmann_as_organization_theorist.

Sidney, Sir Philip. *English Essays*. 27. Vol. 27. 51 vols. The Harvard Classics. New York: Bartleby.com, 2001. https://www.bartleby.com/27/10.html.

"The Literary Estate of Niklas Luhmann." Faculty of Sociology. University of Bielefeld. Accessed February 1, 2021. https://www.uni-bielefeld.de/soz/luhmann-archiv/.

"Thoughts on the Business ff Life." *Forbes*. Forbes Magazine. Accessed February 28, 2021. https://www.forbes.com/quotes/6145/.

Tiago Forte. "Building a Second Brain: Capturing, Organizing, and Sharing Knowledge Using Digital Notes." March 10, 2019. Video, 44:13. https://youtu.be/SjZSy8s2VEE.

Traphagen, Mark. "How and Why I Launched Roam: Conor White-Sullivan on 20 Minute VC Podcast." Roam Tips, May 9, 2020. https://www.roamtips.com/home/conor-white-sullivan-roam-twenty-minute-vc-interview.

Walker, Andy. "5 Mental Models for Investing & Everyday Life." *Augury*. Augury, April 18, 2020. https://www.auguryresearch.com/blog/5-mental-models-for-investing.

Wilson, E. O. *Consilience: The Unity of Knowledge*. New York: Knopf, 1998.

Chapter 11: Mental Models

"#52 Hack Away the Unessentials." Bruce Lee. Bruce Lee Enterprises, June 29, 2017. https://brucelee.com/podcast-blog/2017/6/28/52-hack-away-the-unessentials.

"A Wonderfully Simple Heuristic to Recognize Charlatans." *Farnam Street* (blog). Farnam Street, November 12, 2019. https://fs.blog/2014/01/a-wonderfully-simple-heuristic-to-recognize-charlatans/.

Anderson, Chris. "Elon Musk's Mission to Mars." *Wired.* Conde Nast, October 21, 2012. https://www.wired.com/2012/10/ff-elon-musk-qa/.

Barker, Eric. *Barking up the Wrong Tree: The Surprising Science Behind Why Everything You Know About Success Is (Mostly) Wrong.* New York: HarperOne, 2019.

Big Think. "Julia Galef: Think Rationally via Bayes' Rule." Updated October 8, 2013. Video, 3:22. https://youtu.be/NEqHML98RgU.

"Charlie Munger: The Power of Not Making Stupid Decisions." *CNBC MakeIt.* CNBC, August 4, 2017. https://www.cnbc.com/2017/08/04/charlie-munger-the-power-of-not-making-stupid-decisions.html.

Clear, James. "First Principles: Elon Musk on the Power of Thinking for Yourself." *James Clear* (blog). James Clear, February 3, 2020. https://jamesclear.com/first-principles.

Crabbe, Tony. "Why We're Better off with Fewer Friends." *Quartz.* Quartz Media, October 2, 2015. https://qz.com/515255/why-were-better-off-with-fewer-friends/.

Eliason, Nat, and Neil Soni. "Seek Wealth, Not Money or Status. The Almanack of Naval Ravikant by Eric Jorgenson." *Made You Think Podcast.* Made You Think Podcast, October 26, 2020. https://madeyouthinkpodcast.com/the-almanack-of-naval-ravikant/.

Encyclopedia of Religion. s.v. "Via Negativa." Encyclopedia.com. Accessed January 12, 2021. https://www.encyclopedia.com/environment/encyclopedias-almanacs-transcripts-and-maps/negativa.

Ferdman, Roberto. "There Are 19 Ingredients in McDonald's French Fries." *The Washington Post.* WP Company, April 26, 2019. https://www.washingtonpost.com/news/wonk/wp/2015/01/22/there-are-19-ingredients-in-mcdonalds-french-fries/.

Hayes, Adam. "Peter Principle: What You Need to Know." *Investopedia*. Investopedia, August 28, 2020. https://www.investopedia.com/terms/p/peter-principle.asp.

How Not to Give a Fuck. "Elon Musk On Overcoming His First Fear." Updated October 13, 2013. Video, 0:32. https://youtu.be/suD1aBwwZfU.

Jeffries, Adrianne. "Bottoms Up: The Ballmer Peak Is Real, Study Says." *Observer.* Observer, April 13, 2012. https://observer.com/2012/04/bottoms-up-the-ballmer-peak-is-real-study-says/.

Kachroo-Levine, Maya. "Anthony Bourdain Quotes That Will Inspire You to Travel More, Eat Better, and Enjoy Life." *Travel + Leisure.* Meredith Corporation, February 5, 2019. https://www.travelandleisure.com/travel-tips/celebrity-travel/anthony-bourdain-travel-food-quotes.

Kiecolt-Glaser, Janice K, Timothy J. Loving, and Jeffrey R. Stowell. "Hostile Marital Interactions, Proinflammatory Cytokine Production, and Wound Healing." *Arch Gen Psychiatry* 61, no. 12 (December 2005). https://doi.org/10.1001/archpsyc.62.12.1377.

Konnikova, Maria. "The Limits of Friendship." *The New Yorker.* Condé Nast, October 7, 2014. https://www.newyorker.com/science/maria-konnikova/social-media-affect-math-dunbar-number-friendships.

Kyle, Mary. "Impact of Toxic Relationships on Heart Health." *Empow-HER.* Her Inc, February 25, 2019. https://www.empowher.com/heart-disease/content/impact-toxic-relationships-heart-health.

"Lewis-Mogridge Position." Academic Kids. Accessed March 9, 2021. https://academickids.com/encyclopedia/index.php/Lewis-Mogridge_Position.

Miller, Brendan. "How 'Survivorship Bias' Can Cause You to Make Mistakes." *BBC Worklife.* BBC, August 28, 2020. https://www.bbc.com/worklife/article/20200827-how-survivorship-bias-can-cause-you-to-make-mistakes.

"Mirazur." The World's 50 Best Restaurants. William Reed Business Media. Accessed January 24, 2021. https://www.theworlds50best.com/the-list/1-10/Mirazur.html.

Sims, Maddy. "This Is the Average Wedding Guest List Size in the U.S." theknot.com. *The Knot,* October 1, 2019. https://www.theknot.com/content/average-wedding-guest-list-size.

"Thoughts on The Business of Life." Forbes Quotes. *Forbes Magazine.* Accessed March 9, 2021. https://www.forbes.com/quotes/415/.

Urban, Tim. "The Cook and the Chef: Musk's Secret Sauce." Web log. *Wait But Why* (blog). Wait But Why, November 6, 2015. https://waitbutwhy.com/2015/11/the-cook-and-the-chef-musks-secret-sauce.html.

Urban, Tim. "The Tail End." Web log. *Wait But Why* (blog). *Wait But Why,* December 11, 2015. https://waitbutwhy.com/2015/12/the-tail-end.html.

Wen, Tiffanie. "The 'Law' That Explains Why You Can't Get Anything Done." *BBC Worklife.* BBC, May 21, 2020. https://www.bbc.com/worklife/article/20191107-the-law-that-explains-why-you-cant-get-anything-done.

Chapter 12: The Secrets of Serendipity

Adams, Scott. "Career Advice." *The Dilbert Blog,* July 20, 2007. https://dilbertblog.typepad.com/the_dilbert_blog/2007/07/career-advice.html.

Austin, James H. *Chase, Chance, and Creativity (The Lucky Art of Novelty).* MIT Press, 2003. Quoted in Marc Andreessen. "Luck and the Entrepreneur, Part 1: The Four Kinds of Luck." PM

Archive. Updated August 14, 2007. https://pmarchive.com/luck_
and_the_entrepreneur.html.

Brown, Paul B. "'You Miss 100% of the Shots You Don't Take.'
You Need to Start Shooting at Your Goals." *Forbes*. Forbes
Magazine, January 12, 2014. https://www.forbes.
com/sites/
actiontrumpseverything/2014/01/12/you-miss-100-of-the-
shots-you-dont-take-so-start-shooting-at-your-goal/?sh=
7b17a1cb6a40.

Burkeman, Oliver. "This Column Will Change Your Life: A Step in
the Right Direction." *The Guardian*. Guardian News and Media,
July 23, 2010. https://www.theguardian.com/lifeandstyle/
2010/jul/24/change-your-life-walk-burkeman.

Chesky, Brian. "7 Rejections." *Medium*. Medium, July 12, 2015.
https://medium.com/@bchesky/7-rejections-7d894cbaa084.

Cieply, Michael. "Aside from the Vampires, Lincoln Film Seeks Accuracy." *The New York Times*. May 9, 2011. https://www.nytimes.com/
2011/05/10/movies/abraham-lincoln-vampire-hunter-rewrites-
history.html.

Csikszentmihalyi, Mihaly. *Flow: The Psychology of Optimal Experience*. New York, NY: Harper & Row, 1990.

Duckworth, Angela. "What's the Downside to Being Goal-Oriented?" Produced by Rebecca Lee Douglas. Podcast audio. No
Stupid Questions. Freakonomics, August 30, 2020.
https://freakonomics.com/podcast/nsq-goal-oriented/.

Fater, Luke. "How the Man Who Invented Xbox Baked a 4,500-Year-
Old Egyptian Sourdough." *Atlas Obscura*. Atlas Obscura,
April 2, 2020. https://www.atlasobscura.com/articles/what-
bread-did-ancient-egyptians-eat.

Goldstein, Michael. "Can Airbnb Continue to Grow after IPO
Launches It to $100 Billion Valuation?" *Forbes*. Forbes Mag-
azine, December 10, 2020. https://www.forbes.com/sites/

michaelgoldstein/2020/12/10/can-airbnb-continue-to-grow-after-ipo-launches-it-to-100-billion-valuation/?sh=1d968d441453.

Hajar, Rachel M. D. "Painting with Bacteria." *Heart Views* 18, no. 3 (2017): 108. https://doi.org/10.4103/heartviews.heartviews_105_17.

Kunthara, Sophia. "Turo Adds Another $30M to Series E." *Crunchbase News*. Crunchbase News, February 5, 2020. https://news.crunchbase.com/news/turo-raises-another-30m-to-series-e/.

Limb, Charles. "Your Brain on Improv." TED. TED Conferences, November 2010. https://www.ted.com/talks/charles_limb_your_brain_on_improv.

Oldfield, Philip. "Diverse Parental Genes Lead to Taller, Smarter Children, Finds Extensive Study." *The Guardian*. Guardian News and Media, July 1, 2015. https://www.theguardian.com/lifeandstyle/2015/jul/02/diverse-parental-genes-lead-to-taller-smarter-children-says-extensive-study.

Ravikant, Naval. "Making Money Isn't about Luck." Naval, January 31, 2020. https://nav.al/money-luck.

"Roam White Paper." Roam Research. Accessed February 22, 2021. https://roamresearch.com/#/app/help/page/Vu1MmjinS.

"The Generalized Specialist: How Shakespeare, Da Vinci, and Kepler Excelled." Farnam Street, March 1, 2020. https://fs.blog/2017/11/generalized-specialist/.

"The New York Times Best Sellers." *The New York Times*. The New York Times Company, 2010. https://www.nytimes.com/books/best-sellers/2010/03/21/.

Ward, Alie. "Gastroegyptology (BREAD BAKING) with Seamus Blackley." Ologies, July 7, 2020. https://www.alieward.com/ologies/gastroegyptology.

Zhang, Jenny G. "A Conversation With the Team That Made Bread With Ancient Egyptian Yeast." *Eater*. Eater, August 8, 2019. https://www.eater.com/2019/8/8/20792134/interview-seamus-blackley-serena-love-richard-bowman-baked-bread-ancient-egyptian-yeast.

Chapter 13: Chaos

Ancient History Encyclopedia. s.v. "Heraclitus of Ephesus." By Joshua J. Mark. Accessed February 1, 2021. https://www.ancient.eu/Heraclitus_of_Ephesos/.

Campoy, Ana. "216 Companies on the Fortune 500 Were Founded by Immigrants or Their Children." *Quartz*. Quartz Media. Updated December 9, 2017. https://qz.com/1151689/216-companies-on-the-fortune-500-were-founded-by-immigrants-or-their-children/.

Chanakira, Isaac. "3 Practical and Effective Stoic Exercises from Marcus Aurelius, Seneca and Epictetus." *Daily Stoic* (blog). Daily Stoic. Updated August 8, 2017. https://dailystoic.com/practical-stoic-exercises/.

Clear, James. "How to Stick to Your Goals When Life Gets Crazy." *James Clear* (blog). accessed February 4, 2019. https://jamesclear.com/plan-for-chaos.

Csikszentmihalyi, Mihaly. *Flow: The Psychology of Optimal Experience*. New York, NY: Harper & Row, 1990.

Hawking, Stephen. *A Brief History of Time*. New York: Bantam Books, 1998.

Hoffman, Reid. "M&A Or IPO?" *Greylock*. Greylock Partners, July 23, 2020. https://greylock.com/greymatter/reid-hoffman-ma-or-ipo/

Isaacson, Walter. *Steve Jobs*. New York: Simon & Schuster, 2011.

Levin, Irwin P, Judy Schreiber, Marco Lauriola, and Gary J Gaeth. "A Tale of Two Pizzas: Building up from a Basic Product Versus Scaling Down from a Fully-Loaded Product." *Marketing Let-*

ters 13, no. 4 (November 2002): 335-44. https://www.jstor.org/stable/40216481?seq=1.

McKenna, Terence. "A Quote by Terence McKenna." *Goodreads.* Goodreads. Accessed March 10, 2021. https://www.goodreads.com/quotes/161861-the-creative-act-is-a-letting-down-of-the-net.

Merriam-Webster, s.v. "chaos (n.)." Accessed February 3, 2021. https://www.merriam-webster.com/dictionary/chaos.

Officialpsy. "PSY—GANGNAM STYLE(강남스타일) M/V," July 14, 2012. Video, 4:12. https://youtu.be/9bZkp7q19fo.

"PayPal Holdings Net Worth 2013-2020: PYPL." *Macrotrends.* Macrotrends LLC. Accessed February 7, 2021. https://www.macrotrends.net/stocks/charts/PYPL/paypal-holdings/net-worth.

Potts, Rolf. *Vagabonding: An Uncommon Guide to the Art of Long-Term World Travel.* New York: Ballantine Books, 2016.

"Preserving Optionality: Preparing for the Unknown." *Farnam Street* (blog). Updated March 23, 2020. https://fs.blog/2020/03/preserving-optionality/.

"Steve Jobs on Creativity." *Farnam Street* (blog). Updated November 9, 2019. https://fs.blog/2014/08/steve-jobs-on-creativity/.

Taleb, Nassim Nicholas. *Antifragile: Things That Gain from Disorder.* New York: Random House, 2016.

Thompson, Hunter S. "A Quote from The Proud Highway." *Goodreads.* Goodreads. Accessed March 10, 2021. https://www.goodreads.com/quotes/47188-life-should-not-be-a-journey-to-the-grave-with.

Vandor, Peter, and Nikolaus Franke. "Why Are Immigrants More Entrepreneurial?" *Harvard Business Review.* Harvard Business Publishing, October 27, 2016. https://hbr.org/2016/10/why-are-immigrants-more-entrepreneurial.

Conclusion

"'Artist's Shit', Piero Manzoni, 1961." Tate, Accessed March 1 2021. https://www.tate.org.uk/art/artworks/manzoni-artists-shit-to7667.

Barrowclough, Anne. "The Supernova Hunter." *The Australian.* *The Weekend Australian Magazine*, July 21, 2018. https://www.theaustralian.com.au/weekend-australian-magazine/reverend-robert-evans-star-gazer-and-supernova-hunter/news-story/2f09ed8311093a41795c90d36254429e.

Bryson, Bill. *A Short History of Nearly Everything.* London: Black Swan, 2016.

Houston, Pam. "The Truest Eye." Oprah.com. Harpo, Inc. Updated November 2003. https://www.oprah.com/omagazine/toni-morrison-talks-love/4.

Lipsky, David. *Although of Course You End up Becoming Yourself: A Road Trip with David Foster Wallace.* Google Books. New York, NY: Broadway Books, 2010. https://www.google.com/books/edition/Although_Of_Course_You_End_Up_Becoming_Y/U-8YZLhg7aMC.

Loff, Sarah. "Apollo 11 Mission Overview." *NASA.* NASA, updated May 15, 2019. https://www.nasa.gov/mission_pages/apollo/missions/apollo11.html.

"Thoughts on The Business of Life." *Forbes Magazine.* March 1, 2021. https://www.forbes.com/quotes/1776/.

Wiser, Bill. "Encounters: Supernovae and Revival with Rev. Robert Evans, June 2019." Bruderhof, August 7, 2017. https://www.bruderhof.com/en/voices-blog/world/encounters-supernovae-and-revival-with-reverend-robert-evans.